BEYOND WORDS

BEYOND WORDS

15 WAYS OF

DOING PRAYER

Kristen Johnson Ingram

MOREHOUSE PUBLISHING
A Continuum imprint
HARRISBURG • LONDON • NEW YORK

Morehouse Publishing, P.O. Box 1321, Harrisburg, PA 17105

Morehouse Publishing, The Tower Building, 11 York Road, London SE1 7NX

Morehouse Publishing is a Continuum imprint.

an explorefaith.org book
Spiritual guidance for anyone seeking a path to God

Unless otherwise noted, the Scripture quotations contained in the text are from the New Revised Standard Version Bible, copyright © 1989 by the Division of Christian Education of the National Council of Churches of Christ in the U.S.A. Used by permission. All rights reserved.

Cover art: Charles Neal, Summer, Glos./SuperStock

Cover design: Corey Kent

Library of Congress Cataloging-in-Publication Data

Ingram, Kristen Johnson.
    Beyond words : 15 ways of doing prayer / Kristen Johnson Ingram.
        p.   cm.
    Includes bibliographical references.
    ISBN 0-8192-1973-8 (pbk.)
    1. Prayer—Christianity.   I. Title.
BV215.I54 2004
248.3'2—dc22
                                                        2003027424

Printed in the United States of America

04 05 06 07 08 09   6 5 4 3 2 1

Contents

Foreword

Mother's Bibles fell apart. A Baptist saint, she read, underlined, and made notes in the margins, until the bindings split and the pages fell out. She was faithful in prayer, but Bible reading was the heart of her daily devotions.

Once, when she was in her eighties, Mother asked me, "What is the great book about prayer today?" She was sure that Harry Emerson Fosdick's *The Meaning of Prayer* held the place of honor for Christians of her generation, but she was curious to know what might have superseded it.

I suggested *The Genesee Diary* by Henri J. M. Nouwen. First published in 1976 (and still in print), this modern spiritual classic met the need of Americans coming out of the turbulent Sixties for a refreshingly honest look at prayer, starting with basic questions concerning the possibility of faith.

Along with sharing his own soul's journey, Nouwen made reference to authors of spiritual classics like Brother Lawrence and Bernard of Clairvaux and included modern books like Pirsig's *Zen and the Art of Motorcycle Maintenance* and Pasternak's *Doctor Zhivago*. It was a contemporary attempt at reviving an old, familiar prayer tradition.

Thirty years later, we live in a startlingly different world. The categories and constraints of classic catholic theology have been left behind. There is new freedom of experimentation and expression. The thrust is toward direct experience. Instead of drowning our prayers in a sea of words, we "taste and see" mystery at the heart of life. It's the difference between reading child development books and suddenly having the twenty-four-hour-a-day care of a baby.

In this postmodern world creeds and catechisms give way to gazing in awe at a sky streaked in silver, purple, and red. We kneel not before the shrine of inherited traditions but before the beauty of heavens set on fire. Richard Holloway, former Primate of the Episcopal Church in Scotland, has titled his latest book *Doubts and Loves: What Is Left of Christianity.* The good bishop invites us to join the dialogue, not with arguments and answers but by sharing our stories of sacrifice, forgiveness, and love.

Beyond Words is a guidebook to this new frontier of experiential prayer and spiritual storytelling. Kristen Ingram shows us how to "do" prayer: to dance, sing, walk, skip, listen, see into the very heart of reality. Part shaman, part poet, part priest, her original, lyric approach lights our way into a new realm. We find ourselves praying as if for the first time, praying by doing instead of thinking, by actions instead of words.

When, for example, we watch the Christmas episode of *The West Wing* with her, Ingram hovers over the scene like an unseen angel. She replays the show's fast-paced contrast between a holiday celebration at the White House and a burial at Arlington, then surprises us by calling the TV drama an offering, a prayer. "Watching that five minutes of television," she writes, "said more about God and to God than I could ever pray in words." This caused a shock of recognition in me. Prayer is not limited to traditional venues. Spiritual embers can burst into flame while watching television.

"Taking your disabled neighbor's garbage can in is *mitzvah* and therefore honors God," writes the author of *Beyond Words*. That set me thinking. Our protest marches were a kind of street prayer. The candles we lit in the dark were sacraments. Freedom songs expressed the longing in our hearts for racial justice and peace. "To love another as yourself would be praying," says Ingram. Exactly so.

In one of the most compelling passages of the book, Ingram takes us with her on a first experience of labyrinth, the medieval prayer walk that has been etched on the floors of churches all over America. Walking through a maze-like pattern, engaging in quiet introspection, seekers have been known to have a direct encounter with God. While engaged in this spiritual discipline, the author suddenly blurts out: "I can't make any money writing poetry." The answer she receives sets her on the path of spiritual detachment and true freedom. The labyrinth becomes far more than a prayer walk. It is now the "circle of Presence," her own dance with God.

If you would like to be in conversation with God, entering into the "circle of Presence," you can find no better place to begin than by reading this book.

I suggest you read it slowly, meditatively, no more than a chapter at a time. Give your heart a chance to settle in and your mind space to wander. Burning bushes appear to those who turn aside, not to those who hurry on.

Many years ago, I was rector of an Episcopal church in a community south of San Diego. We had a day school. The author of *Beyond Words* was one of our teachers. This was long before she wrote the first of her twenty published books, before all those magazine and newspaper articles. She was a young mother caught in a difficult marriage, trying to preserve her sanity by doing something creative.

My oldest son was one of her students. David insists that she was the best teacher he ever had. From Kristen he learned to value creativity—his own and others'—and to appreciate art and music. I never understood how she could have such a great impact on his life until I read *Beyond Words*. Now, I think I know. Her teaching was a prayer—a heartfelt cry—that each person's life become an oblation, a spiritual offering, a dance in the "circle of Presence."

When I think of Kristen Ingram, of what she has meant to her readers and to all those students in her writers workshops through the years, I remember these words of Albert Camus:

Don't walk in front of me, I may not follow.
Don't walk behind me, I may not lead.
Walk beside me and be my friend.

I am one of many who have had the privilege of knowing Kristen as such a friend. The readers of *Beyond Words* are graciously invited to join that number. I only wish my mother had lived long enough to read Kristen's book. I think she would have found what she was looking for: an invitation to do prayer.

The Rev. Fred Fenton
Baton Rouge, Louisiana

explorefaith.org books:
An Introduction

The book you hold in your hands says a lot about you. It reflects your yearning to forge a deep and meaningful relationship with God, to open yourself to the countless ways we can experience the holy, to embrace an image of the divine that frees your soul and fortifies your heart. It is a book published with the spiritual pilgrim in mind through a collaboration of Morehouse Publishing and the Web site explorefaith.org.

The pilgrim's path cannot be mapped beforehand. It moves toward the sacred with twists and turns unique to you alone. Explorefaith.org books honor the truth that we all discover the holy through different doorways, at different points in our lives. These books offer tools for your travels—resources to help you follow your soul's purest longings. Although their approach will change, their purpose remains constant. Our hope is that they will help clear the way for you, providing fruitful avenues for experiencing God's unceasing devotion and perfect love.

www.explorefaith.org
Spiritual guidance for anyone seeking a path to God

A non-profit Web site aimed at *anyone* interested in exploring spiritual issues, explorefaith.org provides an open, non-judgmental, private place for exploring your faith and deepening your connection to the sacred. Material on the site is rich and varied, created to highlight the wisdom of diverse faith traditions, while at the same time expressing the conviction that through Jesus Christ we can experience the heart of God. Tools for meditating with music, art, and poetry; essays about the spiritual meaning in popular books and first-run films; a daily devotional meditation; informative and challenging responses to questions we have all pondered; excerpts from publications with a spiritual message—all this and more is available online at explore faith.org. As stated on the site's "Who We Are" page, explorefaith.org is deeply committed to the ongoing spiritual formation of people of all ages and all backgrounds, living in countries around the world. The simple goal is to help visitors navigate their journey in faith by providing rich and varied material about God, faith, and spirituality. That material focuses on a God of grace and compassion, whose chief characteristic is love.

You have the book, now try the Web site. Visit us at www.explore faith.org. With its emphasis on God's infinite grace and the importance of experiencing the sacred, its openness and respect for different denominations and religions, and its grounding in the love of God expressed through Christianity, explorefaith.org can become a valued part of your faith-formation and on-going spiritual practice.

CHAPTER ONE

Doing Prayer

Moses said, "Show me your glory, I pray." —Exodus 33:18

During an afternoon break at a retreat in northern Idaho, I sat on a log and watched a fat honeybee roving around a big blue pasque-flower. She tasted its petals, snuffled at the opening, and then drew back and literally hurled herself at the flower's center. For all I know, that bee is there still, soaking up whatever gifts the flower has to offer.

Like the honeybee, you may feel as if God is luring you to the inner perimeter of heaven. You try to breathe the remote perfume of holiness and sample an unimagined sweetness, but if you want more you'll finally have to hurl yourself at the center—at the place where God is most God, and where you are most yourself. And then you transform your life into prayer. With abandon. As you *do* prayer you can *become* prayer, and fire, and love, and you can then invite God to pray you. When that happens, not only spoken prayer but every moment of art or gardening or music or politics or arguing with your spouse is shot through with God's presence and God's opinion.

You may as well reconcile yourself to the fact that God apparently believes that opinion is more important than answer. God is obviously tilted toward green, brown, oceans, and beetles because that's what we have most of. So if you pray, "Should I become a doctor?" and you hear, "Noticed the basswood tree lately? Seen those June bugs?" you can only assume that your need for guidance isn't as important as your need to acknowledge God's love for the earth. And God's reason may not be clear.

Every now and then, someone brings out a book on efficacious prayer, a sort of "pray to get results." Which we don't always get or see. I've prayed for things that never came true. I've begged God to do things I ultimately had to do myself. And sometimes I've shaken my fist at heaven. Prayers apparently go unanswered sometimes or have miraculous responses at others, and that can make you think God is capricious.

Efficacious Prayer

When I was in my early teens every day I saw a blue neon sign on a nearby church, a sign that flashed, "Prayer Changes Things." I'd like to go back to that church and adjust the sign to say, "Prayer Changes People." I would not be a woman writing this book if I were not a woman who was changed by constant prayer. Prayer made me who I am. I would *like* to think my prayer also changed circumstances and conditions, but until I translated prayer into doing—until, as my Pentecostal friend likes to say—I "put legs on those prayers"—efficacy was indeed out of reach. And is efficacy really all I'm after? Is the measure of benefit whether I prayed and I got?

I think efficacious prayer isn't about getting. What you may want is an answer to a problem, or guidance about a job, or even the right numbers for winning the lottery. But really productive prayer is whatever makes you or me more fit for the Kingdom. Norman Pittenger, the late theologian, author, and seminary professor, said that praying makes you want what God wants.[1] So prayer, whether done or spoken, whether chanted or handsprung or danced, makes people different. A praying person is not like one who doesn't even whisper "Amen." Prayer, if nothing else, is a blessing to the human personality.

A man close to me practices "slogan Christianity," summing up theology in short phrases, lists, and aphorisms. According to this maxim-monger, all human petitions to God receive one of three answers: Yes, No, or Wait. Nicely composed, but his succinct analysis doesn't work for most of us, who are trying to penetrate the enigma of God and to confront the riddle of prayer. His glib statement doesn't help someone struggling to understand why a loved one dies or a job doesn't happen. And such a simplistic explanation of prayer's productivity suggests that the deck is stacked, that every answer from God is already predetermined.

I don't buy it. Thomas Paine, of American pre-Revolution fame, wrote, "The Predestinarians . . . appear to acknowledge but one attribute in God, that of power. . . ."

Paine wrote better than he knew. If God is both unmerciful and unchangeable, why pray? If everything is predestined, if God has already decided whom to favor and whom to reject, marked us before birth for heaven or hell, then the church and prayer are useless. If you reduce God to an angry, violent elder waiting to yell "Gotcha!" then prayer would be neither efficacious nor even reasonable, unless the prayer was a constant "Keep me from sin." And if God is only a wild ball of formless energy, that fireball probably wouldn't have the ability to hear prayers, either, much less grant them.

The Practice of Prayer

Growing up Episcopalian, I didn't question whether prayer worked or not. I prayed out of obedience to God and for love of the language in our *Book of Common Prayer*. I murmured with pleasure "grant us such a lively sense of thy mercies," "we have erred from thy ways like lost sheep," and "O ye whales and all that move in the waters, bless ye the Lord." Eventually I wanted something richer than words, so after I was grown, when the Episcopal day school where I taught began in 1967 to have chapel services from new prayer book revisions, I detached myself from tradition and embraced God's continuing revelation. And finally, I decided to do my prayers besides just saying them.

The truth filters down to earth through many screens and sieves, and I can't know while I'm on earth how valid the truth is about prayer. And that's a good thing. Prayer is—and should be—a mystery, the greatest mystery of all because in it you try to engage the God who is unknowable in ordinary conversation. In prayer you call up the eternal and ask it to be revealed to the finite. Perhaps you whisper the Our Father as you fall asleep, and say grace over your food, and holler "Fix this!" at God when you watch the day's depressing news. But sometimes you can't find words, or you're so mad at God you can't form a sentence. Or maybe you feel verbally inadequate to express your love or anxiety or whatever. Or maybe it's just that the nonrational wins that day. You're not just a mouth attached to a brain: if God made all of you, then all of you needs to learn how to communicate with God, and *doing* prayer responds to that need.

Observant Jews know how to do prayer. Prayer can of course mean recitation, but many devout Jews put the emphasis on *mitzvah,* or a good work. To love another as yourself would be prayer, and so would picking up the oranges that have fallen to the sidewalk at an outdoor fruit stand. You do prayer when you hand twenty dollars to the homeless woman who stands in the median strip, holding a sign. Taking your disabled neighbor's garbage can in is *mitzvah* and therefore a prayer that honors God and your neighbor.

Making Prayer

Converting spoken prayer to doing prayer may start with the need to accompany words by moving the body: bowing again and again while reading Torah, my kneeling and standing in church, a nun bending to light votive candles, an elderly couple raising their hands and arms during praise, or your walking through the dark, ferny woods as you recite the Jesus prayer. When you want to move closer to God, when the "bee of your heart" longs to taste heavenly nectar, you can take the next step and the next thing you know, you're doing prayer.

You may already be doing prayer. Perhaps all you need to do is notice what you do and dedicate that time to God. For instance, one woman had spent a couple of hours in prayer and meditation every afternoon. In the year before she went to seminary, she listened to music and engaged in spiritual reading and contemplative prayer after lunch every day. But during her first months as a postulant she felt absolutely frazzled: she had no free time to devote to her contemplative exercises because she had piles of books to read and papers to write, kitchen duty to help pay for her tuition, and evening discussion groups with other students.

Finally, she realized that reading theology and understanding the Bible and digging into church history *were* prayer So every day when she sat down at the table in her tiny seminary apartment to study, she lit a candle. At the end of her homework, she added a doxology and said "Amen." Not only did she feel better about her prayer life, she began to enjoy study as much as she had loved her afternoon music and devotion. When she graduated and was ordained, she entered the priesthood with increased enthusiasm.

Sometimes doing prayer is intentional, but at other times, you realize during or even after your activity that you have entered into new communication with God. Maybe you were working in the garden, which is one of the most meditative things people do; maybe as you dug your fingers down into dark soil, you whispered, "Oh, look! Red wigglers!" Or "Look! The nasturtiums are coming through the soil!" When you trust the earth to bring forth the seeds you plant, and praise the presence of worms and seeds and insect-eating birds, you've joined God in creation and found another way to do your prayers.

Or maybe you take a walk every day in a place that declares God's presence. I'm as aware of creation when I walk on the nearby logging road in tree-spangled, rainy Oregon as I was when, as a child in Arizona, I hiked beside the saguaro cactus that lifted their arms to heaven, while lizards with blue undersides swifted up the palo verde trees. Every time you acknowledge Creation, you have prayed. Zen Buddhists believe in a strict policy of "mindfulness," in which walking while thinking, taking pictures, listening to a CD is unheard of. When you walk, you pay attention to walking. And although the concepts of Zen Buddhism originated in the East, they are not so different from those of Western mystics. Once a novice found St. Teresa of Avila devouring a partridge, holding the roasted carcass in her hands and ripping the meat off with her teeth. "Well," she told the horrified novice, "when I pray, I pray. When I eat a partridge, I eat a partridge."

Which reminds us that eating and drinking can be holy occupations. So can looking at your environment, or an icon, or a person's face. The prayer of the eye needs no words, because what you see dances straight through your brain and your nervous system and imprints forever on both memory and spirit. Dance and listening to music can all be spiritual activities that you can dedicate to God. In her novel, *Household Saints,* Francine Prose wrote about a young girl who imitated the Little Flower, the saint who gloried in small tasks. That girl was so enraptured doing work for God that as she folded laundry, she stretched her arms out in ecstasy as her arms and hands held the sheets up like huge wings.[2]

Getting Started

You might want to start by making a list of things you *like* to do, and choose one to start your new prayer life. These don't have to be brand-new, untried exercises. Tonight as I sliced potatoes, onions, and parsley into the frying pan and laid a fresh trout below the broiler, I turned my work into prayer. I love to slice potatoes, seeing the faint flowery pattern in their centers. And the rainbow that shimmered on the side of the trout reminded me of God's very first covenant. When I put dinner on the table, I waited until my husband said grace, and answered "Amen" —to both my potato prayer and the one my husband spoke.

But doing prayer can be spontaneous. Today, in the middle of August, I looked out at the big snowball bush that grows by my window. Although its big pompom blossoms have faded and dropped, the dark green leaves now shade the house; and today, the wind moved in them, dappling sunlight on my window and reminding me that the wind bloweth where it listeth. I spread my arms upward like branches in wordless invitation to the Spirit to blow through me, too. So you're as welcome to the wind as I am.

The first step in doing prayer is making your activity *intentional* and *consecrated.* "Intentional" means you decide beforehand what you're going to do and "consecrated" implies that you will commit a sacred act dedicated to God. If you find yourself singing as you walk the dog, you might feel prayerful and God will certainly honor your celebration; but we're talking here about planned worship.

Theologian Matthew Fox says, "Everyone is a mystic." He explains that we were born full of wonder, and can recover that sense of wonder at any time by exercising our awe. So approach your first efforts with delight and expectation. Say to yourself, "This is how I am going to pray," and then begin. Choose an activity—juggling, journaling, painting, poetry, hiking, or haiku, and dedicate it to God as prayer. Before you begin, create a ritual: you could light a candle, or wash your hands, to remind yourself of your baptism, and of the refreshment of living water. Or make a physical motion: place your hands together in front of you in the *namaste*, or prayer position, then bow, genuflect, or take a few dance steps. The hymn "God Be in My Head," is a good one to sing as you start on this journey:

> God be in my head, and in my understanding;
> God be in mine eyes, and in my looking;
> God be in my mouth, and in my speaking;
> God be in my heart, and in my thinking;
> God be at mine end, and at my departing.[3]

Then create or continue an activity, dedicating it as prayer. At the end of your walk or painting or garden work, say "Amen," extinguish your candle, and let gratitude for God's approval fill your heart.

A Prayer for Your New Prayer Adventures

Dear God, please be in my understanding. I'm going to learn a whole new way of praying, and I am both excited and scared. Help me find the kind of "doing" that's best for me. Amen

CHAPTER TWO

Walking into the Fire of Prayer*

He replied, "But I see four men unbound, walking in the middle of the fire, and they are not hurt; and the fourth has the appearance of a god."—Daniel 3:25

People all over the world have for centuries practiced firewalking. But we're fascinated, perhaps because most firewalkers profess a deep spiritual connection to the eight-hundred-degree embers. They say that after their firewalk they feel free and closer to the rest of the universe.

The three young men in Daniel didn't walk across coals; they were thrown into a raging furnace because they didn't bow down to worship the golden statue of Nebuchadnezzer when they heard "the sound of the horn, pipe, lyre, trigon, harp, drum, and the entire musical ensemble" of the palace, as Babylonian law demanded. Shadrach, Meshak, and Abednego were devout Jews who worshipped no king except God, and their firewalking was meant to be a capital punishment for breaking the law.

---

*Portions of this chapter appeared as "The Presence" in *Weavings,* Spring 1999.

But Somebody walked with them, and the flames had no effect on them. They emerged unscathed, and Nebuchadnezzar said the fourth had the appearance of a god. Which he was.

And what does that Bible story have to do with "doing prayer"?

Walking Prayer and Prayer-Walking

To walk as prayer is not the same as to walk praying. You can use a breath prayer or a phrase of Scripture as you stride or stroll, and let it take the rhythm of both your breath and your walking pace, and you will achieve spiritual and emotional benefit.

But to turn walking itself into prayer means heading for the fires of God. The same "Fourth Person" that accompanied the young men in the furnace was a "theophany," or appearance of God. And the same God walks with you, so you move in a state of awe, maybe even trepidation. Do I mean walking scared? Well, not scared, exactly, but with wonder and amazement and reverence, both for the untamed Christ who is walking with you and for the wild earth you tread.

Thich Nhat Hanh, the Vietnamese Buddhist scholar and writer, said in *The Miracle of Mindfulness*, "We have to walk in a way that we only print peace and serenity on the Earth. . . . Walk as if you are kissing the Earth with your feet." That means being aware of where you are, what you're doing, and keeping your intention to make prayer.[1]

Steps on Fire

One late summer evening, I sauntered along the wet sand at the edge of the Pacific Ocean. Big waves broke well beyond me, and rippled out, and occasionally splashed over my instep. When I looked back after the sun had set, my long trail of footprints was glowing in the semi-darkness. I held my breath and wondered at the trace I had left, wondered if I had pulled down a fiery message from God. But then a big comber rolled over my whole pathway, and my dynamic footprints washed away. The foam on the next big wave glowed, too, like hot green fire.

When I went back to our table on the beach, I tried to convince my husband that I was magical, that my shining footprints had set the waves on fire, but of course I knew the phenomenon was the result of phosphorescent algae. Fireflies on land or glowing jellyfish and algae in the sea are bioluminescent organisms that remind us that God is Light from Light, true God from true God, begotten, not made. My footprints on the wet sand had only been a witness to God's glory, not to mine. But I will never forget the sight because I glimpsed something of God's presence in my own steps. Which brings me back to Thich Nhat Hanh, not because Buddhism is superior to Christianity, but because most Christian theologians don't bother to write much about walking and saintly Buddhists do.

Thây (Teacher), as Thich Nhat Hanh's followers call him, says, "People usually consider walking on water or in thin air a miracle. But I think the real miracle is not to walk either on water or in thin air, but to walk on earth. Every day we are engaged in a miracle which we don't even recognize: a blue sky, white clouds, green leaves, the black, curious eyes of a child, our own two eyes. All is a miracle. The real miracle is not to walk on water or in thin air, but to walk on earth."[2]

Contemplation versus Surroundings

So to walk as prayer, I have to be mindful, living in present time, knowing that when my feet touch the earth they should call up the presence of God, should leave the imprint of peace or love or fire. When I leave my office and head through the rest of my house, I can see my laminated cherrywood floors, the red wall in the dining room, the crystal chandelier my husband rescued from being thrown away. But I don't focus on any of those elements: I stay quiet inside, letting my feet move in a state of grace. I am here—not to dominate my environment but to offer it up. I am here as a walking sacrifice, walking into the fire of God's love, and even the house in which I live can shine with that love.

I am lucky enough to have a paved logging road behind my house and below the wooded hillside. I enter the road and soon I am looking down at my roof and the roofs of the neighborhood. I can walk a quarter-mile and then climb up a steep hill to a little fenced family cemetery more than a hundred years old, where six headstones, some broken, lie in dark shadows among the fir trees. I can rest there, and bless the memory of the people who once had a homestead on this reforested land. The presence of volunteer apple trees attest to their history, even though the old house has gone back to the earth.

Or I might keep walking another mile, keep my feet in contact with the planet, and end up down at Wallace Creek Road, which turns toward Fall Creek Dam. Once I might have gone the whole eight miles to the dam but stiff joints and pollen allergies have made that harder. But the length of the prayer-walk isn't critical; whether you take three thousand steps or six, they are sacred. Instead of being trapped in the vortex of emptiness, the whirlpool of commercialism, the push-push-push of the workplace, or in the desert of poverty and despair, you can simply walk, and head into the fire, acknowledging your environment while you let your heart speak to God.

Cougars as Prayer

Once I hadn't cared about his existence and so I never realized how close I probably came to him. I remember a time when I was trudging through the woods and caught a faint, acrid scent on the wind, something like damp fur or some other animal probability. But one morning my neighbor called to say, "We saw the cougar yesterday, down near the old pasture. So keep your little dog and cat in."

Longing for a sight of that cougar overcame me as the days went by and my walk became a cougar search. I climbed the hills and traversed the forest, finding deer spoor and pale, winking jelly mushrooms and blackberry thorns that tore my clothes and ravaged my arms and face. Never had I wanted anything so much. My appetite flagged and my skin grew rough from the ragged kiss of the winter wind as I turned seeking into prayer.

"Perhaps the cougar is also stalking you," my husband joked. *Stalking me?* I didn't laugh at his joke but closed my eyes and felt curved claws ripping into my arms and chest, sensed great teeth sinking into my neck. I felt shaken like a feather duster.

"I'd be willing to die if I could just see him," I said, and then I knew what this had really been about. *I would die to see him.*

I ran to my neighbor's house. "Did you finally see the cougar?" she asked.

"Not yet," I said. "But I was really hunting something else. Someone, I mean."

"Who?

"God," I said. My arms and thighs thrummed with delight and terror. *And maybe God is stalking me.*

"You're looking for God out there in the hills?" Her gray curls bobbed as she laughed. She slapped her knee and shook her head. And then she leaned forward and whispered hoarsely, "Take me with you?"

To Walk Is to Pray

To walk mindfully, to walk with intention, is to pray. You can stroll slowly in your backyard, a step at a time, and kiss the earth with your feet; or you can stride into the wind, looking for mountain lions; or you can shuffle along a neighborhood street under the summer trees, blessing every sprinkler that cools you with its shower. Intention makes walking into prayer, and so does gratitude for what you see, whether it's a house trailer or a redwood tree or the gold imprint a cougar leaves for a moment on the atmosphere.

The earth should be sacred to all of us, and to walk on it is indeed a miracle. To tramp the tree-covered hills searching for God, to skip down a city street reveling in the presence of angels and angels and angels, to caress a country lane with careful feet, to find your inside by going outside: all these are acts of prayer, honored in heaven and worthy in God's sight.

Getting Started

If you already walk every day, you might want to choose a different route for your prayer activity so you can create a new intention. If you can find a beautiful natural place to walk, such as the beach, or a desert in bloom, go there and be aware of your gratitude for Creation. But if you're limited to a city street, a dirt-paved lane with trash blowing around, the halls of a nursing home with slippery floors or the tiled length of a covered mall, then try to see with new eyes so that even blowing trash is transformed into beauty. Watch the light and shadows change on the floor and be aware of the sound your feet and breath make.

So that you won't daydream or forget to be mindful, try breathing in rhythm with your step. You can even use a "mantra," or sacred word, such as "God," or "Peace," if that helps you center in; or use some form of the Jesus Prayer, such as "Jesus, have mercy." If you focus easily on walking as prayer, you can skip the mantra.

Go only as far as you are comfortable; wearing yourself out won't make your prayer-walk feel very spiritual. If you have a bad knee or a painful lower back, just go a half-block or so. You can repeat the same route and routine every time you walk, you can lengthen it a bit each time, or you can try something new each time you walk. Just make your intention clear to both yourself and God, and ask Jesus to walk with you.

Each time you take a prayer walk, write a sentence or two about your experience. You can describe what you saw, but it's more important to write down what you felt: joy, impatience, fatigue, delight, or whatever emotion you experienced and what God told you through your footsteps.

If You Can't Walk

If you can't walk, (or take a wheelchair or scooter down a path) then walk in your heart. Walk in memory or imagination, and let God's warmth pour down upon you. Maybe you can drive (or be driven) to a beautiful park, or a quiet country lane, or a long, peaceful beach where the tide rolls in under a dark blue sky. Take some picture of the place: if your photos are digital, you can pull one up on your computer screen or your television, and mentally walk the route. And if you're lucky enough to have a camcorder, maybe you, or a family member, could videotape a whole walk down a road or path or seashore.

If all those suggestions are impossible, subscribe to a travel magazine and let it suggest your walking route. Ask friends for scenic postcards when they travel. And above all, enjoy your prayer-walk even if you take it from your chair. Let your imagination or memory guide you so that eventually you can tell that Someone is walking with you.

A Prayer for Walking

I'm walking with you today, God. Stay close to me and don't let me wander away from you. Let me really kiss the earth with my feet. Amen

CHAPTER THREE

Walking the Sacred Circle

He has described a circle on the face of the waters, at the boundary between light and darkness. —Job 26:10

Candles flamed and flickered at the cross points of the four spirals, and a soft recording of Gregorian chant created a holy mood. As I set my stocking foot onto the path, where several other people moved in various positions in the labyrinth—beautifully inlaid in the polished floor, in several kinds of wood—I felt tears spring to my eyes. I'm not a person who cries in public or even often alone, but I forced myself not to fight my tears. They came and went several times....

Now that you've started to walk your prayers, you may want to join me in a labyrinth walk. A labyrinth is another way to bless God and the world with your feet. But don't just think "walk"; instead, start contemplating pilgrimages into a holy land. To walk a labyrinth is to make a pilgrimage externally *and* internally. When you traverse the laid-out paths, whether they're in perfect quadrants or looser meanders through trees or around buildings the experience is more important than the destination. The experience is one of wordless prayer, sometimes intense and tearful, sometimes filled with pure joy. I've tried to analyze what happens in a labyrinth, but I can't. The answer lies below the level of words. If you surrender to the Holy Spirit's imperatives, you're alone in the labyrinth, no matter how many others are on the swings and swoops nearby. You're silent until you all have completed the circle. You leave what you take into the labyrinth at the center, either as a gift to God, or as a burden surrendered; and you bring out a different gift because God is always showering them down.

Maron, my spiritual director, told me about her powerful labyrinth experience at a retreat center and suggested I try one. I'd walked a labyrinth before, but I'd felt silly and self-conscious, so now I brushed the idea away. But as I sat with Maron over coffee and scones, she simply described her own experience to me and offered a couple of gentle nudges. She told me about the special labyrinth walk, with candles and music, at our cathedral. And she recommended that I read *Walking a Sacred Path* by Lauren Artress.[1] I ordered the book and decided to give the labyrinth another try.

Where Did Labyrinths Begin?

A labyrinth is not a maze. It has no tricks, dead ends, or blind alleys. Although the path circles first one way and then another, your feet are always moving inward to the center and, later, outward toward the beginning. Mazes, on the other hand, usually don't have centers. With intersecting paths , dead-ends and cul-de-sacs, they are constructed to challenge the mind, while labyrinths nurture the spirit.

A few occasional responses to labyrinth walking of "New Age!" surprise me, since the labyrinth most often copied is inlaid in the floor of the Cathedral of Notre Dame at Chartres, constructed more than seven centuries ago. Labyrinths have a long and respected tradition in Christian spirituality, but their history goes back even earlier, to the days before Christ.

Archaeologists have uncovered labyrinths and spiral walking designs in ancient sites, along with "finger labyrinths" etched in stones of temples and holy places. The most notable path was in the

Minoan palace on Crete, where a meandering series of halls and chambers finally led to the bull-god, or Minotaur. The structure and its imitators are called *Cretan,* or classical seven-circuit labyrinth. So much a part of the fabric of this early society was the labyrinth that it was embossed on coins and pottery.

The tradition found its way into the new world even before the Europeans found our continent. The Hopi, a southwestern nation of Native Americans, used symbols of the emergence into this layer of earth that look like a seven-circuit labyrinth—but they use two forms, and one of them is square! The same paths and turns are involved, but the corners are square. One is painted red and the other orange, and because they use both shapes, both masculine and feminine principles are involved. A combination of the two forms is also carved on a wooden stick which is planted in front of the One Horn altar in a Hopi ceremonial kiva at Walpi, Arizona, during a yearly ceremony.[2]

Early Christian labyrinths date back to the fourth century: notable is a basilica in Algeria, where the words *Santa Eclesia,* or Holy Church, are inscribed at the very center. In Italy there is a ninth-century wall labyrinth at the St. Lucca cathedral; Christians traced the pathway with their fingers. The labyrinth has always been a sacred path, an ancient symbol that spoke to our spiritual ancestors of their pilgrimage here on earth. With only one path winding throughout the symbol that they walked or traced with their fingers, the pilgrims often experienced the labyrinth as a mirror for their own lives.

Celtic and other British Christians continued to use spiral designs in their worship as well as in priestly jewelry and clothing. But the Middle Ages in Europe brought the design of the labyrinth into church again. Crusades and pilgrimages had added energy and purpose to the church from the eleventh century onward, but they were usually activities of the wealthy: contemporary piety held that if a man participated in a crusade or financed one, or sent his servant to fight the enemy, his sins could be forgiven. When the papal court fell into financial trouble, the rich were allowed to donate money instead.

But that left out women and the poor. Women in medieval Europe couldn't march into battle, and poor people couldn't raise an army, but the desire to embark on a pilgrimage was so strong that churches began to create holy places and shrines much closer to home. But the farmer with fields to tend, the woman with a brood of children who needed her attention, and the poor tradesman who worked every day couldn't leave home and walk to a shrine forty miles away. So churches created small shrines and finally labyrinths to represent pilgrimages. The best-known (and perhaps the most complicated) labyrinth design in the world is copied from one inlaid on the cathedral floor at Chartres, France in the thirteenth century. The Chartres design is a classical labyrinth with eleven concentric circles and the rose design at the center as a twelfth.

According to historians, the labyrinth at Chartres was created for Easter celebrations during which the dean of the cathedral would dance into the center, followed by the congregation, in a symbolic act of Christ's death and resurrection. The center was the garden tomb, and resurrection happened as they danced out. Christians lost this tradition as well as use of the Cathedral labyrinths as spiritual and meditative tools, due perhaps to the Reformation or the Enlightenment, or both.

Psychologist Lauren Artress, an Episcopal priest and counselor at Grace Cathedral, San Francisco, used labyrinths as early as 1985 as an instrument of spiritual development. Artress had been searching for a spiritual tool or pilgrimage experience for late twentieth-century Americans. The people who came to her led active, stressful lives that left no time for classic spiritual disciplines of prayer and meditation. When they faced the death of loved ones, divorce, career changes, or severe illness, they didn't have the spiritual strength to support themselves, let alone others who depended on them. So Artress began to use the labyrinth as tool to promote their healing and spiritual growth.

Now labyrinths are everywhere. Chances are you live not too many miles from a church with an inlaid or outdoor or canvas labyrinth, and most of these are available to anyone who wants to walk them. Some churches, like Trinity Cathedral in Portland, Oregon, where I began the pilgrimage I described at the start of this chapter, have regular "walks" with candles, flowers, and quiet music.

When I prepared for my first visit I told Victor, my sixteen-year-old grandson, that I would pick him up after school and take him with me, and convinced my husband Ron to go, too. I attended my writer's group, collected Victor, and raced home for my husband to find that the labyrinth book had arrived and my husband had picked up sandwiches for our supper. I read during the two-hour drive to Portland, sometimes silently and sometimes aloud. We arrived at Trinity about six, and a smiling woman in the entry showed me a map of the labyrinth, mentioned that it turned and twisted just as life did, and directed me to go on into the hall, take my shoes off, and enter the circle.

As I began the walk I began to hear God talking somewhere deep in my mind. As I looped over to the right side, I heard God telling me to write more poetry; as I looped to the left, I heard God talking about my upcoming presentation to a Lutheran synod in New Jersey.

"I can't make any money writing poetry," I told God.

"Oh, well, if money is what you want, it's outside," God said. "Money belongs to space and the things that occupy it. You're enclosed in time, here; step out of the circle if you want space instead."

It was St. Paul's "law of perfect freedom," suddenly made clearer to me. I can either dance in the circle of God's love, or settle for what the world offers. I can't walk both roads at the same time. "All right," I said, as I looped to the right again. "More poetry." And then, "All right," I said, as I looped to the left. "I'll organize my addresses to the Lutherans." Back and forth I went, in and out, arriving one by one at the four lighted points of the Cross, where I felt impelled to bow and thank God for being my Father and Mother, and to thank Jesus for being my brother.

Finally I was at the center, and I sat down in one of the petals of the rose shape in the middle. Three or four other men and women were in the center, standing or kneeling or sitting. Victor arrived shortly after I did, and he sat down in the lotus position. I think I knelt and I heard the Great Silence, a silence that is not empty but filled with divine presence, a silence from which all the music of the world pours, a silence in which God speaks the eternal Word.

I finally forced myself to start walking outward. I knew something profound was happening to me, but I couldn't put words to it. Although I was following lines, the meaning of the labyrinth is non-linear, non-rational. As I stepped out of the last circle, and onto a little oriental rug, I picked up and rang a pair of soft brass bells.

I sat awhile on an incongruous folding chair, looking at the whole picture: labyrinth, walkers, dancers, candles, high ceilings, all. Eventually my husband and grandson came out and sat in silence. I watched a woman in a long dress dance and twirl her way through; bells were sewn into her skirt and they rang softly like those in a Buddhist monastery. A man wearing a prayer cloth walked so slowly I could hardly see him move.

"I'm going again, if you can wait," I told Ron and Victor. The second time was faster and I didn't feel as many tears; this time, I was caught in the whirlwind, and I let it move me where it would. This time the lessons of the first experience became more integrated and perhaps imprinted on my mind. It was the same experience, but more reinforcing and less revealing.

Afterward, we ate our sandwiches out on the church patio by electric lights. The night was magic, with a perfect half-moon rising, Venus the next-brightest thing in the sky, and the scent of autumn on the breeze. We were thirsty, so we stopped for gas and cold drinks; as I got back into the car, I caught sight of the book, lying on the car seat. In the yellow half-light, the labyrinth design looked like something I'd seen before.

It looked like a "PET" scan, like the two hemispheres of the human brain.

I had walked my own brain, my own consciousness. Poetry and joy on the right side; enough organization to speak to the world on the left. Mary, Martha, and all the shades of being, in between. The doer in my right hand, the dreamer in my left, opposite of the brain sides. I had walked and looped and stood in the center, in the middle between the fire and the knowing. I had reconciled my brain to itself; I had come home to my center. I felt as if the scattered parts of my life had converged within.

Now my own church has an outdoor labyrinth, created by parishioner Mike Van, a well-known Northwest artist, and a crew of high school kids and local homeless people who were not only glad to earn a little money, but who contributed artistry and spiritual strength to the design. Our beautiful, woodsy outdoor Celtic knot meanders in a way the tight Chartres labyrinth does not, because we didn't want to cut down the oak and fir trees in our big churchyard. In the daytime, sometimes after church, many of us traverse the path. In moonlight, the plants and boulders that shape the walk glimmer silver and you can even hear the quiet calling of the deer that live in our parish's little forest grove. Whatever I take into the labyrinth I leave in the center, sometimes laying down a burden, and at other times offering God a sacrificial gift. At the center, my pilgrimage is only half done; as I walk out, I remind myself that I have really left my gift or burden behind, in the care of Jesus Christ. Christ, who stands invisible at the center, carrying us inward, and then sending us out in peace to love and serve one another as faithful witnesses.

Next time I walk a labyrinth, I'll look for you. Maybe I'll wear a long skirt and big earrings. I might even sew on some bells.

Getting Started

Unless you live somewhere very isolated, you can probably find a labyrinth nearby. Many churches and religious institutions have permanent inlays or labyrinths on canvas. A number of Internet sources are available, to help you find a circle near you, or even to let you "finger-walk" a labyrinth. Some of those resources are:

Georgetown University Labyrinth Site
http://www.georgetown.edu/labyrinth/labyrinth-home.html

Grace Episcopal Cathedral
http://www.gracecathedral.org/labyrinth/index.shtml

Grace Episcopal Cathedral Labyrinth Locator
http://www.gracecathedral.org/labyrinth/locator/index.shtml

Sacred Labyrinth
http://www.angelfire.com/tn/SacredLabyrinth/

A Prayer for Labyrinth Walking

Lord Christ, your life on earth took many paths and roads. Enter the labyrinth with me and let me experience the circle of your presence. Amen

One Step at a Time
A labyrinth poem by Suzanne Moody

Rows of ragged rocks outline a path for healing?
Brown, decaying leaves hug the winter ground—a blanket
  to transform?
The labyrinth awaits the sojourner—
almost calls her name—
Will you enter my simple boundaries
and journey my paths
One Step at a Time?
Straight ahead, yet winding and crooked
The curled road beckons to be trod—
reinforcing the uplifted
blessing the downtrodden
Maybe tears, maybe joy, maybe peace
One Step at a Time.
All who are heavy laden, come stand at the gate
All who are fragmented, place one foot down
and the other in front
All who find wonder in the commonplace,
Come travel the narrow rows
One Step at a Time.
Give up your burdens, your middle of the night worries
Lay a care on a silver, craggly rock as you pass
and move on to the next,
the monotony will soothe you
One Step at a Time.
Moving inward,
The trail winds in and out
Muscles untensing,
The walker's job seems easy,
The cares tumble down
and hit the ground with imagined force
lightening the load on contact
One Step at a Time.
Step 48, step 49, many more follow
while curling toward center like a

snail into its shell Motionless at last,
a wooden cross is sighted,
God's presence overwhelms
and envelopes the inner sanctum—
His peace now a cloister
on the journey half over
One Step at a Time.
The pause to discover
new perspectives to ponder
fresh eyes, lightened heart
the world is a wonder
with steps unencumbered
the pilgrimage rewinds
One Step at a Time.
The breathing is slower
the feet touch down lower,
and easier on the road well-worn
The unknown, now familiar
the end is the beginning
the sad is now glory
All happening unexpectedly
One Step at a Time.
A twist inward
A transformation outward
A fresh view from fatigued eyes
All part of a simple design
of much complexity
with the whole greater
than the sum of the steps
All the while traveling
One Step at a Time.

—Suzanne Moody, March 1999, Macon, Georgia[3]

CHAPTER FOUR

A Prayer the Dancer Does

Praise him with tambourine and dance!—Psalm 150:4a

Dance is perhaps the most ancient form of prayer. Long before spoken liturgies, native peoples leapt and moved to drums or other instruments to show their devotion to God. In the book of Exodus, Miriam, Moses' sister, picked up her tambourine and led the Israelite women in a dance of thanksgiving after safely crossing the Red Sea on foot. David danced before the Ark of the Covenant as it came into Jerusalem. And God promised Israel that she would dance as part of divine restoration when Jeremiah prophesied, " . . . O virgin Israel! Again you shall take your tambourines, and go forth in the dance of the merrymakers." And as recent a band as Three Dog Night charges us to dance to music as celebration of life.

Dervishes, Sufi Muslims who wear wide-swinging white shirts and cone-shaped hats, began their whirling rituals around the thirteenth century. They're mystical dancers who say they stand between the material and cosmic worlds. Their dance is part of a sacred ceremony in which they rotate in a precise rhythm, representing the earth's orbit of the sun. Whirling, the dervish empties himself of all distracting thoughts, allowing the music to place him in trance; released from his body he conquers the sensation of dizziness.[1]

After she lights the Sabbath candles, an Orthodox Jewish woman dances with her hands, circling the candles and drawing their light into herself. She covers her eyes in secret prayers, and turns her face upward, perhaps to let God's greater light shine on her. This brief dance follows a different kind of movement: a holy day of cooking and cleaning and preparation. In some Hasidic and Sephardic traditions, she and her family (or sometimes only the men of the village) rush out to the east of their homes and streets, to greet Shabbat as if she were a woman. In much Talmudic literature, the Sabbath takes on a personality and is said to be a manifestation of *Shekinah,* a visible manifestation of God.

When my husband and I were in Jerusalem, we rode a bus through both old and new city on a Sabbath day, and part of our journey was through the Hasidic neighborhood, where the way of keeping the law is descended from the Pharisee sect of Jesus' time. Hasids don't mingle with Christians or Muslims, or even with other Jewish sects. They've been known to spit on modern Reform Jews; they never speak to women who are not their wives and daughters. You might recognize them by their ear locks, black hats, and bushy beards. They're not approachable, and if you see a Hasid on a bus—where they would stand rather than sit beside a non-Hasid—he will look pretty grim and uncompromising.

But as our bus came to an open square, we saw where these Jews were going on a bus. Probably forty men were there dancing with the Torah scrolls, their faces ecstatic. I mentally recorded their smiles and laughter because no matter how rigid or disapproving they look, they love God and celebrate God's story in the Torah. I'll especially remember one man who threw his head back in laughter and song, while on one foot, he turned around and around in a dance of life.

Another activity that combines dance and meditation is tai chi. Tai chi literally means "moving life force" and its choreographed movements are a kind of slow, graceful dance. These forms were designed to mimic animal movements, such as those of the snake and the white crane. Because tai chi requires concentration, some people describe it as meditation in motion. And since those who practice tai chi must relax with each new movement, the "martial art" becomes more a dance than a set of calisthenics. The philosophy of tai chi suggests that when one person achieves harmony with the universe, the entire world is on the path to peace. And when you practice tai chi, you center yourself in God. Tai chi is especially good for people who have some movement limitations or need a no-impact routine.

I love tai chi. I often put together my own movement routine as I walk through my house or stand alone on my back patio. Although I don't think words of prayer during the movements of *chi,* or power, I have a strong sense of communion with God.

Almost all community colleges or adult education programs offer tai chi classes for both beginners and advanced students.

Liturgical dance is taught and performed in Christian churches all over the world. In the written history of the church, dance appears and ebbs. We know such dance was present in the early church because in the apocryphal book the Acts of John we find a hymn the people sang while Jesus led the disciples in a dance.

But because dance was also associated with pagan religions, both the mystery plays and dance waned with the Reformation. The real use of dances as art form, though, is only sporadically present in the history of the church. In medieval times, there were circle dances; there were also labyrinth or mystery dances in the church, and now the practice is showing up again.

Congregations and seminaries have discovered the value of dance as prayer, and are creating liturgies that incorporate either choreographed or spontaneous physical movement. Among the scores of seminaries that offer liturgical dance are Wesley Theological Seminary in Washington D.C.; Episcopal Theological Seminary of the Southwest in Austin, Texas; Columbia seminary near Atlanta; Church Divinity School of the Pacific in San Francisco; and Union Theological Seminary in New York.

Divine Dance

The Sacred Dance Guild promotes dance and ritual as an affirmation of the divine. According to Iris Stewart, dance is divinity and puts the dancer into a state of grace and reunites the body with the mind and spirit.[2]

Another proponent of sacred dance, Christy Edwards-Ronning, says, "With dancing feet and shining faces, we proclaim a life-giving message of salvation, as did the bounding messenger of Isaiah. We are invited to love God and proclaim God's deeds in dance."[3]

I saw prayer danced at the consecration of the new home for the Spiritual Life Institute, a Carmelite monastery in Colorado. Under the big yellow-and-white tent that sheltered the week's activities, a nun exchanged her tan-and-white habit for a leotard and tights and she danced Psalm 139. The audience held its breath as she created the psalm with her motion, her expression, and her graceful hands. At one point she stood on her hands and—to the delight of the audience—cried, "Hesychasm," which refers to the state of silence and inner devotion pursued by cloistered nuns and monks, and others who engage in contemplative prayer.[4] The applause at the end of her performance was punctuated by cries of "Praise God!" and "Hurray for hermits!"

But to dance prayer is not only to celebrate. Every Good Friday in Eugene, Oregon, a slender blond woman dances the sadness of the occasion.[5] She is a former ballerina whose movement conveys grief, even despair, but ends with hope when she kneels in prayer before a wooden cross standing against the altar rails. The congregation is rapt and sometimes moved to tears; her dance is not only a prayer but a sermon about Jesus' crucifixion and death. No words could convey so much sorrow; nor could the angry accusations of stern preachers bring a greater sense of fault to the congregation: they end the service by singing the words, "'Twas I, Lord Jesus, I it was denied thee: I crucified thee."[6]

Dancing Your Prayers

Walking let you move your body as prayer, and the labyrinth made it possible for you to structure motion as a pilgrimage. The next step—literally—is dance, which presents a chance to express joy or celebration or even sadness in Christ's presence. Body movement can reflect mood or even, as in ballet, tell a story. When you dance, you tell your story to yourself so it can be clear to you. When you allow your body to move freely you reflect God's story, too.

Episcopalians, Roman Catholics, and Lutherans may already take their souls through the slow dance of the Eucharist, kneeling, standing, genuflecting, making the sign of the cross, walking forward to receive the body and blood, walking back to the pew, standing for the last hymn. Perhaps you never thought of it as choreography, so I invite you to consider it that way the next time you attend a Eucharist service. Watch the movement around the altar *after* the communion, when the deacons or lay readers and acolytes are moving around with the chalice and paten, the priest is washing the dishes, someone is putting the service book on the altar. What you see will have much in common with a dance movement.

If you attend a more enthusiastic, perhaps a Pentecostal, denomination you may find yourself doing the Tabernacle Two-Step with arms raised and feet moving with delight. I sometimes visit a wonderful church with mostly African-American parishioners who shout, answer, and often get up to dance in little circles, either alone or in groups, during prayers, sermons, and music. When I leave that church the exuberant dance has made me feel as refreshed as a garden after rain.

But you don't have to go to church or to a dance studio to dance your prayers. You can dance in your living room or in your backyard, alone or in company. You can leap with enthusiasm in your worship, or you can just sway a little with a bowed head, either in awe or as a confession of sin. Dancing your prayers isn't only about celebration, but an expression of your whole life. You can worship God by dancing in silence or moving to an African drum or stomping to rock 'n' roll.

As always, *intention* is the key. Decide in advance that your dance, however short or long, and in whatever form, will be prayer. Before you start to dance, you might like to create a sacred atmosphere: you can light a candle, set out a bouquet, open the Bible, or wear a cross on a chain to symbolize that this is a devotional event and that this is your gift to God. That doesn't mean that the place where you're standing—or dancing—is profane until you make it holy. Every atom of the earth is already made sacred by God's participation in its creation, and by the divine presence that pervades all prayer. The reason for the candle or other symbol is to help you focus on your movements as prayer. No human being can make a place holy: we light our candles only to recognize that holiness is here.

Dancing prayer should always be a free, even an abandoned, experience. Whether you're an eighty-year-old with arthritis or a healthy twenty-something, let the dance control your body, not your body the dance. Dance without restrictions or preconceptions of what constitutes a dance. Think of your dance as a "trance," a state removed from the rational. In Kabbalah, the mystical branch of Judaism, the letters *lamed lamed hey* stand for the dream state, in which humans can access the very real but unseen dimensions beyond the physical universe.[7] Why? Because God is more and more present as we travel to deeper spiritual locations, beyond the Bible and the altar, perhaps into the company of God's saints and messengers—who, we hope, are also dancing with us. In dance, you plumb the depths of your soul, and consecrate yourself to God.

Staying alert to your intention is important, but if you get swallowed up by the movement, don't worry. Maybe, at first, singing one of the names of God as you dance will help you keep some focus, but don't restrain your love of movement by anxiety about why you're dancing. God loves the dance, and sent it as a gift to humanity. All you're doing is offering it back. Music will be the focus of Chapter Six, but for now, think about the sounds only in their relation to your dances. Choose any kind of sound that inspires or excites you, from the Beatles to Beethoven. Most people like strong rhythm in their dance music, and I always recommend drumming records of any kind: Asian, Native American, African, or Eskimo, especially if they also include the sounds of bells and timbrels. Or you might buy an inexpensive tambourine, or some brass finger-cymbals that can *tink-tink-tink* your prayer-dancing into audible form. Try to stay away from music that's too martial: you want rhythm but not obedience to the music's quality, and marching probably won't create a sense of prayer. I like to light scented candles and burn incense when I pray-dance. A Christmas carol proclaims that "incense owns a deity nigh" and God is certainly near you when you're pouring your mind and body into any kind of prayer activity. You may dance a prayer or two as you walk through your house, or set aside some time for the activity. If you plan, make sure you've chosen "dance clothes": apparel that's comfortable, non-restrictive, and maybe even a little colorful.

Remember that paisley cape you've kept ever since college? Or the little bells from the labyrinth?

Albert Einstein said, "Human beings, vegetables, or cosmic dust, we all dance to a mysterious tune, intoned in the distance by an invisible player."[8] So as you dance your worship of God, you may accidentally stumble into the Great Dance of heaven. The galaxies are dancing, sometimes moving from one another and sometimes pouring themselves into a neutron star or black hole full of dense energy. The earth dances, moving with the tides, the soft or terrible winds, earthquakes, and volcanoes. And of course, the earth spins and orbits the sun. All matter is dancing, alive, electrons orbiting nuclei, gamma rays and beta particles and sunlight and dust motes: Creation is always on the move, and when you dance you join Creation's praise of its creator.

The pestilence is spiritual: if you need to move or dance or act in some worshipful way, you may feel numb or slothful until you obey that nudge from God. So get up and start dancing.

Getting Started

After you have recognized your space as sacred by lighting a candle or setting up some other symbol, put some music on. The music can be anything you choose, but you *do* want it to help you connect to God. That doesn't mean it has to be a hymn; just use whatever will speak to your spirit about God's Spirit.

Your arms and hands may find it easy to move expressively. So you might want to walk while you wave your arms or turn them into snakes or birds' wings to music or drumming; eventually you'll find your hips and knees joining in. Even if you have physical disabilities, you can probably sway or rock or just move your head to the music.

You might feel silly or self-conscious at first, dancing by yourself. Try to imagine a thousand dancers around you, or concentrate on being in God's sight; and just keep moving. Different kinds of music can make that easier for you. And remember, when you dance alone, nobody judges your performance.

You might also like to engage another person or two in prayer-dancing. You can become a little weekday "church" where you invent your own worship.

Try to dance for a few minutes every day for a week. I guarantee that if, at the end of that time, you don't feel freer or happier, you can have your old mood back.

A Prayer for Dancers

O God, you set the stars to dance over the skies, and the planets to waltz in their orbits. Because I have the dust of the stars in my bones, let me join that eternal dance. Amen

CHAPTER FIVE

Sacred Hearing

Then the Lord said to Samuel, "See, I am about to do something in Israel that will make both ears of anyone who hears of it tingle.—1 Samuel 3:11

No one hears the cry of the poor or the ringing of a wooden bell.—Haitian proverb

God commanded Israel to *listen:* "Hear, O Israel: The Lord is our God, the Lord alone. You shall love the Lord your God with all your heart, and with all your soul, and with all your might" (Deuteronomy 6:4–5). That verse, which has been repeated to Jews for at least three thousand years, is called the *shema,* the call to listen. Ears are both an instrument of prayer and one more way to remember God. They're always "on," even when you sleep. Only the ravages of old age or disease can shut down your ability to hear, and you can pray by listening any time you want. The wind rustles through the trees, frogs sing into the evening, and crickets and cicadas praise God aloud on warm summer nights. But hearing other sounds, including music and voices and even the roar of engines on the freeway can become a prayer any time you want.

Auditory processing is the term used to describe what happens when your brain recognizes and interprets the sounds around you. Humans hear when energy that we recognize as sound travels through the ear and is changed into electrical information that can be interpreted by the brain.

Albert S. Feng, professor of physiology, biophysics, bioengineering, and neuroscience at the University of Illinois, is a renowned expert on the way we process auditory information. By observing frog behavior and then looking at individual cells in the brain, Feng showed that the midbrain processes the information from the ear, so when you listen as prayer, your midbrain springs into action. But other areas of the brain are activated as well, as the electrical impulses of neurotransmitters rush information's electrical impulses around your brain and body. Hearing is more than the brain's processes: when you hear something and give that sound your attention, your whole person is involved.

Start with Music

Almost any kind of music can place me in the presence of God, even the hardest rock or the wildest Schoenberg. I even have a few favorite commercials because I love the backup music. There's the one with Vivaldi's *Four Seasons* and the one with David Bowie telling us to ch-change and an awful, unforgivable commercial whose only redeeming virtue is a great tenor singing "Vesti la giubba" from *Pagliacci*.

I don't have to *think* prayer when I play my scratchy old 33 recording of *Amahl and the Night Visitors*. Just hearing the Melchior's "Swifter than lightning he shall soon dwell among us," and the mother's reply, "Oh, no, take back your gold. For such a king I've waited all my life!" still makes tears spring to my eyes, and what's more important, sends me soaring toward the throne of God. That brilliant opera, with its powerful spiritual message, is available on videotape through Amazon.com.

Straight to Heaven

Secular operas are prayers for me, too, if only for their beautiful sound. At the end of *La Boheme*, when Rodolfo cries, "Mimi . . . Mimi . . . Mimi!" I almost pray for her to live, because he's singing from a deep place inside himself, a place of sorrow—and we all know that place. When years ago I saw famed Wagnerian soprano Kirstin Flagstad sing the *Liebestod*, or "Love Death" in *Tristan und Isolde*, just before her retirement, I expected God to appear as a Valkyrie (I know, wrong opera) to swoop down and take her straight to heaven.

And remember that even a tune whistled by a passerby might send you through the invisible membrane that separates heaven from earth. I can almost hold hands with a seraphim; and sometimes I think I hear an angelic chorus, when I'm between waking and sleep, hear them singing with everything from harps to vibraphones. If I sit up or turn on a light or move the dog off my leg, the choir is gone. But it reminds me that all music surely originates in heaven, and is carried by those same angels from God to composers. I love to imagine angels with blowguns, whooshing the music into the ears of musicians who then try out the tunes that have suddenly entered their brains.

How to Listen

If you want to start with music, use the kind you love best but don't try to pray a song you associate with something else, such as your wedding or a longtime relationship, or music that's so lively it belongs to a party more than a prayer. Try out everything: if you devote yourself for a half-hour every day for a week, you'll run across what makes you aware of God's perpetual presence and grace. If you don't have a player, find the radio station or cable channel that carries the kind of music that you consider best for your prayers.

You can sit to listen, or dance around, or lie down to hear your prayers: but *don't* use the music as background for something else. This is not a time to balance your checkbook, eat cookies, thumb through a magazine, or peel potatoes. Listening to the music *is* your devotion, not its accompaniment.

I think the two hardest things for us to do in the twenty-first century are to sit still in contemplative prayer, and to listen to music without any other activity going on. If we associate music with parties, we can keep boredom at bay while we work or drive. People talk and eat and work out while their DVDs play, and they shove a CD into the player while they negotiate heavy traffic. Fewer and fewer people attend classical concerts, and at most rock events, people stand on their seats, dance, sing, or fall into mosh pits, so the experience is more physical than spiritual. But we apparently hate just sitting down to listen. So you may have to start small, with three minutes or even one minute of listening prayer. Light a candle, burn some incense if you like, then sit, kneel, or stand to listen. Let your soul soar or sink with the music; let the sound beg, praise, or thank, and when you start to fidget in earnest, turn it off. Keep up this program until you can pray-listen for about twenty minutes. Or longer, if you grow to love this process, as I think you may.

Nature's Noises and the Sounds of Yesterday

When I was a little girl on the high Arizona desert, I fell asleep at night listening to the howls of coyotes, and I usually woke up to the call of mountain quails and mourning doves. Even today, the sound of howling makes me feel safe and cozy, as I was in my childhood room. I also loved going to my grandmother's little farm. Not only did I hear her roosters crowing and hens clucking, but the neighbors' cows and goats filled the air with song, and the pastures were full of Western meadowlarks who, I am certain, sang out "William Lloyd Garrison." I enjoyed hearing Nana call "Chick, chick, chick" and the hard scatter of grain on the ground when she fed the poultry.

Think back to your childhood: what sounds come back to you? Your mother's voice, your cat's meowing, the lawn mower in the back yard? How about the church choir? Crickets on summer nights, or frogs singing after the spring rain? How about the horns of taxis, the rumble of buses, and lonely train whistles? Pick out the sound you loved best, and bring it up into present time. Linger in that sound for a while, putting yourself back on the grass in your childhood yard or your bedroom or the tree branch where you sat to read or think.

If you can, separate those sounds from what was going on in your life. Childhood is never really easy, and yours may have been unusually hard. But even in the midst of turmoil, you liked some sound that your environment provided. The chirps of a robin or bobolink, or the wind in the pines, or the pounding of the surf at high tide served to brighten your early morning or ease your falling asleep. So if you want to use that sound as an experiment in listening your prayers, try to keep the sound pure and your negative experiences at bay.

And maybe those sounds made your life happier: I used to argue with my mother every day, and some mornings I headed for school wiping away my tears. But in the wintertime, when the cold wind blew through the pinnacles of our mountains, those mountains *sang*. Even when the Arizona wind blew pebbles against our legs so we walked to school backwards, we loved the deep *hoooom* and the high-pitched *hummmm* that sang through Apache Leap, the pink-pinnacled rock structure that created our skyline. I used to say that someday I was going to compose an opera based on those sounds; I didn't know then I'd write a book about how the song of our mountains made me feel happy even after a fight with my mother.

But if your childhood anger or terror or sadness won't unwrap itself from the sounds that accompanied them, then make your listening prayer an unspoken plea for comfort or safety. Prayer doesn't have to be joyful: God wants to hear your prayers of fear, anguish, or any kind of emotion connected to a sound. And you may even find that as you call up an old sound, you can experience, along with God's gracious comfort, forgiveness toward someone who hurt or angered you in childhood.

Although we love the sounds of nature, they can sometimes become disordered or even frightening. I haven't lived through a hurricane, but I've been in a number of earthquakes, some of them severe, and I'll never forget the time when the ground seemed to roar along with the waves of chaos that swelled and buckled the streets. I was close to a tornado once, and my brain still contains the sound of the wild wind and the siren that pulsated through the city. But even the memory of those terrifying sounds can be the centerpiece of prayer. If I never got scared I wouldn't need God very much, would I? Just calling up that earthquake's rolling rumble sends me flying to God's bosom.

I used to be in a parish that offered a "listening retreat" every summer, on a beautiful tract of forest and ferns, with access to a lake for swimming and boating. In those days, it contained a couple of run-down buildings, one of them a house with a kitchen.

Even though our accommodations were sparse, we loved listening. We heard, and joined in, songs and hymns. Those of use who brought guitars or autoharps played them into the night. We listened to preaching and teaching, and during the days we hiked or strolled through the ancient Douglas firs and alders, with sage-green moss hanging from the trees and ferns rustling around our ankles. The sounds were amazing: we could hear the creek tumbling over stones, and the crash of a small waterfall. The site was like a wildlife sanctuary, with every kind of bird, from the goldfinches that cry, "Potato-chip, potato-chip," to the big ravens that warn other birds of our coming. And one of the most startling calls was the husky bleat of an elk, probably calling her fawn out of our path. Our listening was prayer: we forgot everything else except listening to the sounds of the forest and lake, and to one another's voices, and to the message God delivered every moment of the retreat.

Sound is always available as a form of prayer. During the wet Oregon winter, an early-morning bird makes the saddest call I've ever heard, a doleful, down-sliding *tweeeooo*. I always imagine him clad in nineteenth-century black mourning clothes, his tail coat drooping and his hat pulled down. But the bird is actually a beautiful varied thrush, with a deep persimmon breast like a robin's, and a necklace of black splotches. He should have an angelic song, but all I've ever heard is his sorrowful morning chirp. And I always laugh aloud, thanking God for the gift of laughter and the presence of birds. Have you listened to the flamingos' unceremonious honks? A well-known writer who was my parents' friend once said he thought a gorgeous bird like a flamingo had no business making such a sound, and they should all be de-voiced.

Live in the Now

What sounds can you hear right now, as you read? They may include cars going by, or dogs barking, or a radio. At this moment, I can hear CNN droning in the other room, and also the sound of my husband muttering at the elected official being interviewed. I hear a leaf-blower outside, and a siren far away. Every now and then one of the tiny green tree frogs that inhabit my yard croaks, sounding as if he weighs three hundred pounds. And at the other end of the house, my cleaning lady is vacuuming the bedroom. My so-called quiet home is actually full of sound. So I start my prayerful listening by separating them. When I listen to the vacuum cleaner alone, I am grateful that I can have a cleaning person because I'm more decrepit than I used to be. She needs my prayers because she feels helpless, and victimized by her ex-husband, and she's without many resources. So I'll make listening to the vacuum's drone a prayer; without words, I can lift that sound to God for the young woman's sake.

I have fifteen wind bells, all but two of them outside. I love to sit on our patio and listen to the deep gongs and high tinkles that the breeze plays in them. And one hanging above my front porch is a wooden "chime" that clacks and whispers its message to my prayerful listening. The sound of wood swinging and touching reminds me of the wooden cross on which Christ handed me my salvation. The first "bells" were probably wooden and I have encountered ones like them in both Zen and monastic Roman Catholic meditation rooms, where the sound of wood doesn't startle.

At the beginning of this chapter, I quoted a Haitian proverb that says, "No one hears the cry of the poor or the ringing of a wooden bell." Well, *does* anybody hear the cry of the poor? *God* does, and says so over and over in Scripture. Proverbs 21:13 warns, "If you close your ear to the cry of the poor, you will cry out and not be heard." The whole book of the prophet Amos is about neglecting the needy. So your listening needs to take a different tack if you want to serve your less fortunate brothers and sisters. Listen to what they ask for (or read it on their signs), and respond. When you hear Santa's bells at Christmas, donate to the Salvation Army. Go to a local soup kitchen and help serve, and listen closely to what people say as you hand them their tray.

What I'm Looking For

In October of 1988 I was standing in mud in Portland, Oregon, when God spoke to me. My son and I were in a college sports arena, waiting for our presidential candidate to arrive. Because we were precinct captains, we should have had bleacher seats, but interlopers had commandeered them, so we stood in the trampled muddy grass. I felt the heels of my blue leather shoes sink into the earth—fashionable, uncomfortable shoes I wouldn't normally wear to stand in the mud. The candidate was two hours late; the governor and congresspersons had already spoken and were grouped on the stage, and the crowd had begun to mutter. Black clouds moved lower, threatening to rain again.

Finally, someone on the event team came to the microphone. "We're gonna play some recorded music while you wait," she said, and I looked with anxiety at the huge speaker only a few feet from me. And then Bono's tight voice began to sing *a capella* the lament that he had climbed mountains, swum oceans, and still hadn't found what he was looking for.

My son said, "Oh, listen," so I listened and heard a real African-American gospel choir echo that *they* haven't found what they were looking for.

"They're Irish," my son said. "U-2." He had tears on his eyelashes. The sky began to shimmer with possibility and then God spoke and I knew that what mattered wasn't when the candidate arrived or even if he got elected; what mattered wasn't that I was standing in mud; what mattered was that I still hadn't found what I was looking for. It wasn't "don't *know* what I'm looking for," because what I was not looking for were political candidates or elections or anything else earthly. What I am always *really* looking for is a chance to see Christ, face to face. And I began to sing softly, sing with Bono and The Edge's guitar and the Victory Gospel Choir and half the people in the arena, began to sing, "I still haven't found...."

The candidate arrived by helicopter. Rain fell on us. I was spiritually and emotionally removed, singing my song under my breath. I saw the presidential hopeful as through the wrong end of a telescope. I felt the rain on my sweater and skirt, knew my hair was slipping from its smooth pageboy into masses of little curls, knew my blue leather high heels had sunk all the way into the clay. But it didn't matter then, or now, because I'm still singing along with Bono and the choir. I know what I'm looking for.

And later I read an interview with Bono in *Rolling Stone*. The tall Irish rocker was asked about his world view, and he said, "I believe that Jesus Christ is the Son of God." So if your kids are listening to U-2 up in their rooms, just shut the door quietly and smile.

To listen is to pray. Perhaps you want to hear music, or maybe attend to the city's noises, or stroll through a wetland to hear the birds. Whatever you choose, listen with your heart as well as your ears. Let yourself be grateful or happy or even scared when you listen. And above all, don't forget to laugh. God created laughter for our joy and his. So listen for a silly frog or a scolding bluejay, or even a clowning piece of music for your delight. You may even hear the source of holy laughter on television: several years ago a Wall Street commercial started with roosters, getting off the subways, rushing up the street, all of them looking purposeful as they came together. Combs and wattles shook and shimmied, and beady black eyes looked around for the right direction. Probably a hundred thousand roosters. As the sun slipped above the dark New York canyon, they all crowed at once. What an amazing sound! I loved seeing the birds put their heads back and open their beaks to crow and the noise of joy and raucous welcome made me laugh out loud.

Getting Started

Take your journal and go to a natural place: a park, a pond, a clearing in the woods, a desert scene, or just a back yard. Listen. What sounds do you hear? Birds, wind in the trees, the rocks shouting in a running creek? Do you also hear cars, helicopters, and other human-made sounds? Without judging which ones are "good" sounds and which are more negative, try to separate them and listen to each. List the sounds in your journal, and a word or two describing your feeling or reaction to it. You may be surprised at what you hear and how it makes you feel. And above all, you can use your hearing as prayer, lifting not only your ears and minds to God, but also your hearts.

A Prayer for Listening

Incarnate Word, without you was no thing made. Let me hear as you hear and care as you do. Amen

CHAPTER SIX

Making Music, Making Prayer

By day the Lord commands his steadfast love, and at night his song is with me, a prayer to the God of my life.—Psalm 42:8

A bird does not sing because it has an answer. It sings because it has a song.—Chinese proverb

I know the Bible because I was a childhood stutterer.

You don't stutter when you sing,[1] so I sang a lot as a kid. I sang the multiplication tables and the eight uses of the objective case. I sang to my parents and sometimes to my teachers, and somewhere along the line developed a fairly reliable mezzo-soprano voice placement. So then I began to sing in earnest.

I learned to sing *lieder* and cantatas and when I was seventeen I joined an oratorio group to sing Handel's *Messiah* for the first time of what would become many. We sang Haydn's *Creation* and Handel's less-known oratorios, such as *Esther, Saul, Samson,* and the horrifying *Jephthah.* And when I sang *The Saint Matthew Passion* by Bach, my life was changed. Music sucked me in and kept me near God's heart.

Bach's setting brought the passion of our Lord home in a way that reading the Bible never could.

And while I was learning to sing, I was also getting serious about my relationship with God. Sometimes after high school classes were over I would even drop by the church to pray before taking the bus home (in those days, Episcopal churches stayed open all the time, and they displayed the wonderful "Enter, rest and pray" sign). When in my thirties I began to read the Bible in earnest, I discovered that I was already full of Scripture. I knew verse after verse after verse, story after story. When I read, "Surely he has born our griefs," I could respond with "and carried our sorrows." My whole body already knew "For unto us a child is born," "Behold, I tell you a mystery," and "Since through a man came death, by a Man also came the resurrection." I could recite "Worthy is the Lamb that was slain," and the great *Amen* from Revelation. Music, song, became my ticket to the holy place.

So my stuttering led to singing, and my singing to the Bible. But that doesn't mean that anyone who wants to sing their prayers has to join a Bach and Oratorio society. The idea is to use song as worship, but the choices have to be yours. You can stand in the shower and sing all parts of the sextet from *Lucia* or warble something by Mick Jagger, or kneel at the coffee table with a hymnal in front of you. Once more, it's all about *intention.*

Singing on Purpose

The Old Testament, especially in Exodus and Leviticus, makes the expression of intention perfectly clear. A rich man should give the Lord a lamb; a poor one could sacrifice a pair of doves or a couple of pigeons, as Mary and Joseph did in Luke 2:22–24: "When the time came for their purification according to the law of Moses, they brought him up to Jerusalem to present him to the Lord (as it is written in the law of the Lord, 'Every firstborn male shall be designated as holy to the Lord'), and they offered a sacrifice according to what is stated in the law of the Lord, 'a pair of turtledoves or two young pigeons.'" Nobody was too poor to make an offering, and intention was acceptable on a sliding scale. If a family was so rich that their tithe couldn't be transported easily—a flock of sheep, say, or twenty bulls, or tons of grain, or many barrels of wine—they could convert their holdings into money and take that to the festival place. There, according to Deuteronomy 14:26, the family could "spend the money for whatever you wish—oxen, sheep, wine, strong drink, or whatever you desire. And you shall eat there in the presence of the Lord your God, you and your household rejoicing together." Strong drink usually meant distilled wine, so rejoicing might have come easily. Meanwhile, a poorer family brought flour and oil, and at the festival they baked tortilla-like cakes and ate them as a duty to God. The feast was a thanksgiving, and eating was an offering. It wasn't about how much you had, it was about mindfully using what you had to glorify God.

Intention is *giving as much as you can.* Jesus praised the intention of the poor widow who had only a penny to drop into the temple treasury; because she gave all she had, hers was the better offering. Whether your voice is like Oscar the Grouch's or you sound like Charlotte Church, sing. Dedicate your song to God and sing praise, sing *tra-la-la,* intone the Lord's Prayer or belt out a canticle. You can hum a wordless song or even stay on one note if that's your best; just remind yourself that your song is to God's glory. St. Augustine is credited with saying that "one who sings prays twice." Whether you're tone-deaf or an opera star, using your voice in song is a celebration of prayer.

One of the best moments in the Episcopal Eucharist is when the celebrant says "join." In the preface to the Sanctus and Consecration, the priest says, "Therefore we praise you, joining our voices with Angels and Archangels and with all the company of heaven, who forever sing this hymn to proclaim the glory of your Name...." And the peoples' response is: "Holy, holy holy...."

Join! We don't invent or initiate the awe-inspiring "Holy, holy, holy, Lord, God of power and might." We *join* a song that goes on in heaven all the time. Eternity is filled with the sound of angelic choirs, all glorifying God; when we sing the words of the Sanctus, we join them. In fact, I think that when you sing anything with the intent of glorifying God, you're joining the company of heaven: thrones, principalities, cherubim, seraphim, dominions, virtues, powers, and of course the angels and archangels. Your voice—monotone or soaring soprano or bullfrog basso—is made perfect and on pitch when it becomes part of that heavenly choir. Your hymn-singing in church or your yodeling in the shower can marry heaven to earth: song becomes the link. Just as my stuttering led me to the Bible through a number of odd steps, so singing the glory of God can send all of us on the journey to God's presence.

A non-Episcopalian friend of mine attended a Sunday morning service at my parish and afterwards asked why, *why* we sing every verse of every hymn—how come Episcopalians sing every word? Because we know how much singing matters, I told her. We find three references to the Virgin Birth in the Bible, but two hundred fifty-four to singing and songs. If a major article of our faith gets only three mentions, then singing must be pretty important to spiritual life. And then there's that matter of the words of hymns: because of their impact, I can't get through "My Song is Love Unknown" or "The Call" without at least a tear in my eye, and I've seen my whole church rock out on "I Am the Bread of Life," lifting their reluctant Anglican hands as they sing, "And I will raise them up."

I spent many formative years in a church that sang everything from "Amen" to the Creed. The Epistle and Gospel were chanted, and we also sang the response, "And also with you." Those of us in the choir learned fancy, technical amens and a descant to every canticle for the year. We processed into the church singing the Venite, and closed the service with the Nunc Dimittis. The only spoken words were the sermon, and I think the rector—who wrote the preface to this book, and who has a wonderful voice—would have liked to sing that, too.

And I have to express my love for the old 1940 Episcopal Hymnal as well as newer ones. Several of them lie on the music rack of my organ, and though change can be hard—I think the compilers were dumb to remove or change the tunes to fine old hymns like "Ancient of Days" or "Drop, Drop Slow Tears" from the 1982 Episcopal Hymnal—I like the progress of our music.

A wonderful choir and a huge pipe organ can make you, like Handel when he wrote the "Hallelujah Chorus," think you've seen the gates of heaven swing open. But to sing yourself is even better, because that means worshiping with your voice, "praying twice." Several times I've been on a prayer vigil in a church, and if I'm alone, I usually open a hymnal, kneel down, and start singing the first hymn and continuing through the allotted time.

In many non-liturgical churches, "worship" means "singing," perhaps because the Holy Spirit seems to be so present during commu-

nal song. While *The St. Matthew Passion* changed my life, Graham
Kendrick's renewal song, "Amazing Love," makes me draw in my
breath, astonished at Christ's atoning work. Although worship
through song alone isn't our weekly worship style, I love attending
such a service once in a while, singing the words over and over until
God has a chance to erupt inside us.

But God isn't just a huge maw that sucks up praise and adoration; the greater benefit is for the one who prays. When you sing,
you don't just lower your blood pressure and regulate your heart
rate; you also make yourself holier, more removed from a crass
world, more dedicated to becoming like Christ. And singing doesn't
have to be "Christian" to delight God. Devout lovers of Jesus also
chant the Hindi words "Om mani padme hum" as a spiritual exercise that not only pleases God but illuminates the singer; and some
people like to sing "in tongues" or even nonsense syllables when
they pray through music.

Pray with Your Instruments

"It's easy to play any musical instrument," J. S. Bach said. "All you have
to do is touch the right key at the right time and the instrument will
play itself." My exasperated piano teacher first relayed that quote to
me when, as a ten-year-old, I was struggling to play one of Bach's
two-part inventions. "The notes are simple," he shouted, and I
answered, "But I'm not."

I was right. A thousand pieces of my brain and neurotransmitters
and experience were involved with my musical performance. I always
had an unsatisfactory lesson after I fought with my mother or had a
bout of asthma, which was often. But once I gave a brilliant performance on a harpsichord, playing the *Goldberg Variations;* another time
I had an awful time playing a simple piano accompaniment for my
daughter's flute recital. Hardly anybody can depend only on their
technique and virtuosity.

But praying through music isn't about performance, because your
only audience is God, whether you play a pipe organ, blow on a cat-
tail stalk, or put a CD in the player. If you play an instrument, you can
easily make music to God. The medium doesn't matter: whether you
play bluegrass fiddle, Bach fugues on a grand piano, or folk songs on

a harmonica, to make music a devotion honors God. Church organists do it every Sunday, and you can do it, too. Create the prayer atmosphere and start playing. Improvise if you like doing that, or play something you know. God doesn't care about styles or genres .

Getting Started

One kind of musical prayer-doing that people need no introduction to is singing. So make your song different in some way: go to a new place, like the beach or a grassy hilltop. Or sing a hymn you've never heard. Or take a familiar pop tune and set the words of a psalm to it.

Take your guitar or flute to the backyard or the beach or sit in your kitchen, and play your heart out, literally: let the music send your heart out to God. Sit at your piano and if you only play the blues and play by ear, pound out your adoration in a B. B. King piece. Lift it up to God, and God will bless you in.

But singing is something you can also do all day. When you're at work, sing softly as you walk to the copy machine or as you go down the stairs to lunch. Walk to a farther bus stop and sing all the way. Sing while you make dinner and of course, *always* sing in the shower. You can't light a candle in there but you can set fire to your musical prayers.

A Prayer for Making Music

God, you are not only our Father, but our Mother. You have sung us to sleep and comforted us with music all our lives. Amen

CHAPTER SEVEN

The Prayer of the Eye

Have I really seen God and remained alive after seeing him?
—**Genesis 16:13b**

Once I was lying on the forest floor, trying to shoot a picture of a wild calypso orchid that waved above a thick mat of moss. I nudged my macro lens to the right setting and was about to click when I noticed, through the magnifying lens, some tiny white flowers on the moss, flowers invisible to the naked eye. They were so pearly, so perfect, unseeable except to one another, that I began to weep with awe and gratitude for the secret blossoms I had seen. I hadn't planned to have such a sacramental moment, but every time I think about those tiny invisible blossoms, my heart is flooded with gratitude for their being there, and for God's allowing me see them.

Your prayer today might lie within a black rock on the pale beach or a painting of Jesus or a tiny bird, fallen from its nest, its parents screeching and swooping.

To pray with your eyes means seeing intentionally, seeing what's around you with new vision, and looking for things and events you've

never noticed or witnessed before. With reverence, you can turn your
eye into a vehicle for prayer.

Edna St. Vincent Millay's 1917 poem "Renascence" (rebirth) speaks
of self-limited seeing: all she could see—or was willing to see—were
three mountains and a bit of forest. She soon realized she could touch
the sky and finally sank into the earth, only to be resurrected through
faith defined in a flowering apple tree.[1]

So before you're ready to see your worship, you may need to exercise your ability to *see*. Begin by looking for patterns: in shadows, the
different shades of green on a forested hill, the reflection that the glass
in a chandelier or light fixture makes on the ceiling. Look at patterns
in a zebra's skin, a willow branch, or the veins in your legs. Try to see
what isn't obvious, what makes a bright color brighter—like green
against rose in a billboard—or whatever sight makes your soul
respond with joy. And ask God to teach you to see, and then to teach
you how to pray through what you do see.

Your Vision Full of Prayer

Seeing your prayers endows everything in your line of vision with
holiness. Whether you peer through the window in a toy store or
gaze down into the Grand Canyon, the spiritual architecture around
you is filled with angels. And God is present wherever you look
because there is no molecule inside you or in your environment where
God is not. Christ's body, which is the "all in all" of Ephesians 1:23,
is described in the New English Bible as "filling the universe," and
Jeremiah 23:24 says, "'Do I not fill heaven and earth?' says the Lord."
Whatever you infer from those verses, you can feel certain that
Christ is present. In the hymn known as the "Breastpiece of St.
Patrick," you affirm that Christ is in front of you, behind you, above
you, below you, and in the mouth of friend or stranger. If Christ is
in a stranger's words, then he is also in your own eyes, to give you a
new kind of vision.

You need not be a "visual learner" to prayer-watch. Like many writers, I absorb information best through my ears and I sometimes have
trouble mentally imaging a scene or object. But God has taught me to
look and to worship with my eyes, and I hope I can see for the rest of
my life. I hope you, too, can find every moment an opportunity for

prayer, can see some element of prayer from the time you open your eyes in the morning until you shut them at night (and sometimes even find yourself seeing those prayers in your dreams, too).

Sometimes my seeing-prayers are spontaneous and at other times I like to plan my practice of this kind of prayer. I set aside a time to go for a walk down the street, or to drive to a park where I can see a waterfall, or to watch kids' faces at a playground. If you're artistic, you might take your sketchbook along as you look at arched windows in a steepled church, or at the flowers that grow by your porch. Go to a museum and look at a painting you've seen many times, but this time look for a juxtaposition of colors you've never noticed, or the structure of a figure or object, or the mood or the message that the painting conveys.

But sacred seeing can also be accidental, too, and you might find yourself surprised and amazed by the prayer that your vision opens up to you.

Looking with Gratitude

Gratitude is often the center of a prayer of the eye, especially when the person praying is looking at nature. A bright rainbow against dark clouds can make your day better, especially when you remember that the rainbow was God's first covenant with humanity. I have a crystal wind chime hanging in my west-facing bedroom window, and in the afternoon, rainbows dance all over the walls and bedspread and carpet. If I walk through the room then, I usually murmur either "Thank you," or "Hello, God." If God has a color, it's rainbow; and those arcs are mentioned in Revelation as a description of the throne, and the color surrounding an angel.

Sometimes an afternoon trip to the bedroom is more of a pilgrimage, a purposeful journey from my office at the other end of the house, to see the dancing rainbows all over the place. In that case, I usually kneel awhile; sometimes I reach my hand out to "hold" one of those shining rainbows on the palm of my hand or stand still to let twenty prism rainbows rest on my body; and I take strength from them. I even wonder if a rainbow could be a hologram of God. Did you know that when you fracture a hologram—a three-dimensional image reproduced by a split beam of a laser, and which you probably see on your credit cards—every shard contains all of the original? So maybe all those little crystal refractions are all dancing pictures of God. Rainbows everywhere, shining through crystals, are intimations of divinity, whether they're confined to the sky or dance on the walls of your bedroom.

You've no doubt looked at cloud pictures all your life. Now train your eye to find prayers in more clouds, but also in reflections and light-play on walls and streets. Watch the way new seasons change the length and direction of your shadow as you walk. Look at the way a pond reflects the landscape above it, and observe the pattern of raindrops against a window.

When I was about five, my grandmother crocheted a bedspread for my mother, an ecru masterpiece with stars and "popcorn." I have it on a curtain rod above and behind my bed and when the room is lighted, I like to peek beneath the edge of the spread to see the patterns the light makes between the stitches. I love the way brightness dances through the trees in summer and creates an exciting design on the black asphalt streets. And when I minister the chalice at communion, I'm ecstatic when I can see the altar cross reflected in the wine that someone's starting to drink.

Let your eyes' prayer sometimes take place in front of a mirror. Smile, frown, and show all the expressions you usually show the world. Then see yourself at a deeper level. What does your appearance say about who you are (or who you want to be)? If your skin has begun to age, look at every small wrinkle with gratitude for your maturity and wisdom, acknowledging God's presence in every moment of your life. Take a dance step to see if that makes you smile, and before you leave the mirror, fold your hands as in prayer and bow to your magical reflection. Or use the breath-prayer directions of spiritual writer Thich Nhat Hanh: "Breathing in, I calm my body; breathing out, I smile."[2]

In wintertime, when we have a lot of rain in Oregon, the occasional sight of sun on the snow-covered Sisters Mountains, extinct volcanoes a hundred miles away, makes me want to sing. I'm always grateful to God for those mountains and all the Cascades range, and for all the natural events here: miles of dark green Douglas firs, babbling brooks and rushing rivers, and enough birds and flowers to keep a naturalist busy for life.

And when I travel to other places, I'm constantly in thanksgiving
for what I see. Last fall, I stood in a little eighteenth-century churchyard in southern New Jersey, where a hundred people were buried—
and I found I was related in some way to about seventy of them. The
red autumn leaves scurrying past my ankles, the American flags on
the graves of my ancestors who were Revolutionary patriots, the
exquisite white clapboard church built in 1741, where I sat in my
foreparents' brass-plated pews, all rose up to create a collage of delight
and a prayer of gratitude. I knelt beside the grave of my great-great-
great-great-great-grandfather, who left England so he could practice
his religion, and I realized that this man, all those men and women,
who came here for their faith, were part of my personal cloud of witnesses. That day, my eyes taught my heart gratitude for hours.

Can Television Become Prayer?

My eye and spirit are awakened and turned toward heaven at the
opera, and at art gallery openings and anytime NBC reruns its first-
season Christmas episode of *The West Wing*, titled "In Excelsis Deo."

The scene flicks back and forth between the President's listening to
a children's choir—surrounded by poinsettias and candles and White
House staff, dressed for Christmas—and the bleak Arlington honor-
guard burial of a homeless veteran, attended only by the veteran's
slow-minded brother, the President's secretary, and Toby, the White
House communications officer. All on a bright, cold Christmas Day.
At first, you only see an ordinary children's choir, singing *The Carol of
the Drum* a capella, but as the hearse pulls up in Arlington, an orches-
tra begins the relentless bass *rum*-tum-tum, *rum*-tum-tum of the
carol, and the children's voices turn into something like the Vienna
Boys' Choir. The lonely, homeless Korean-war hero is laid to rest and
the honor guard fires its rifles between the notes of the Christmas
carol. Arlington Cemetery is bright and cold and impersonal, while
the White House is warm, darkened except for candles and the actors'
faces. *This is the world in conflict with God,* this scene makes me think.
Watching that fifteen minutes of television said more about God, and
to God, than I could ever pray in words.

When television first showed me the World Trade Center buildings falling, my soul leapt into prayer, crying out and begging for

mercy. Over and over, the networks showed the scene of the buildings falling, relinquishing their long residence in Manhattan. I kept thinking they fell as if bending their knees in genuflexion, telling the horrified onlookers that at the end, humanity's greatest achievements can be thrown on the fire like grass. I made myself look at anguished faces and flag-covered stretchers and weeping firemen, because prayer, like life, isn't always fun and also because intercession is our highest calling. You don't have to say words for every intercession because if you're looking with your spiritual eye at someone's tragedy, your mind will shoot those arrow-prayers into the heavens.

During that terrible September morning in 2001, before the buildings fell, I saw two people on the ledge of a window with flames from above and inside licking the air around them. They turned to each other and joined hands, then jumped. I sucked in my breath, and I know God interpreted that gasp as prayer, because right away I felt comforted, knowing that those two people, who helped each other face death, were surely welcomed into the Kingdom. And their taking hands before they jumped was their prayer. I suspect they called on God until they lost consciousness either from shock or from striking the pavement ninety floors below; but their joining hands to comfort and encourage, deciding that death from falling was better than death by fire, was a spectacular movement of faith.

Television is both the best and the worst of our experiences. Last night, I accidentally watched at least eight moments of murder and brutality within a twelve-minute span of a movie we had rented before escaping to the bedroom to read. But television has also brought me the entire Wagner Festival from Bayreuth, something I could never afford to attend. God's hand is on all the media: the print press, radio, television, and even the internet. I try not to watch dramas full of violence, but I am willing to look at scenes of terror from New York or Jerusalem or Baghdad, because God uses my eye to form my spirit and I need to contemplate the sorrow of others to become a three-dimensional Christian.

Looking disaster or death in the eye can be a powerful prayer. When my neighbor was dying of cancer, I sometimes sat beside him, silently gazing at his face, trying to absorb his pain and sorrow and uncertainty. He was scared, so I tried to feel his fear, hoping that then he wouldn't have to experience it. But my feelings of fear weren't as important as my looking, because I have now memorized the face of pain. My eyes have taught me compassion and God has given me more than one opportunity of this kind. Christ calls us every day to end suffering, to cast out the demons of fear and ignorance and hunger where we find them. I must see with my heart as well as my eye.

I love the words of al-Ghazzali, the eleventh-century Sufi teacher: "Your heart is a polished mirror. You must wipe it clean of the veil of dust that has gathered upon it, because it is destined to reflect the light of divine secrets."[3]

Getting Started

You can make a formal start, planning your day of seeing as prayer; or you can just add intention into your normal routine. Try the mirror exercise I mentioned as you get ready for work, and glance at the furniture and other objects in your home with gratitude.

Start by seeing the world as blessing. You'll find disaster or despair soon enough, but God's intent toward us is always beneficent, and the natural world existed without sin for several billion years before we appeared on the scene. So begin by seeing God's love in everything from that black rock on the beach or in the front yard to a parhelion, that rare rainbow that occasionally appears as a ring around the sun. Then journal at least an occasional list of "prayers I saw today."

A Prayer for Seeing

God of all beauty and truth, grant me the ability to pray through what I see, and reveal to me the places and people and objects where I'll find your presence. Amen

CHAPTER EIGHT

Gazing into Mystery

Your eyes will see the king in his beauty; they will behold a land that stretches far away.—Isaiah 33:17

Now you no longer see darkly as in a mirror. You have developed the prayer of seeing, so now you may want reach more deeply into the prayer of the eye, into the place where God is less rational and a lot more mysterious.

One important way is gazing at an icon. I found out why in the ancient Church of Our Savior at Karye, outside Istanbul, Turkey, in its original fresco of *Anastasis* (Resurrection). You've seen reproductions of it in art books: Jesus, in gleaming white raiment, is pulling Adam and Eve out of their tombs. Adam and Eve have looks of shame that barely hide their secret surprise and delight. They'd dwelt for thousands of years in Sheol, where other souls were shadows and nothing moved around them—until suddenly Jesus pulled them upward into the light.

Before then I had never engaged in icon or picture meditation, but the faces and rhythm of that fresco caught and held me for at least twenty minutes—in fact until my husband touched my shoulder and said our tour bus was leaving. After that I knew something about God I hadn't known before. And I found something new about my hope in the Resurrection.

Icon meditation? Isn't that just for monks of the Orthodox Church? No. Modern Christians often avail themselves of the practice and look into the mystery of God's love. Praying with an icon means you crucify your intellect and allow the non-rational, mystical side of yourself to emerge. Doing prayer, where icons are concerned, means *not* doing: don't put words to prayers, don't try to think why the image is important, don't attempt to rationalize anything. St. John Damascene said, "The beauty of the images moves me to contemplation, as a meadow delights the eyes and subtly infuses the soul with the glory of God."[1]

Well then, what about the edict against "graven images"?

Ephesians tells us, "He has abolished the law with its commandments and ordinances, that he might create in himself one new humanity in place of the two, thus making peace." If we didn't believe that the law against images was abolished, little girls wouldn't have dolls, church windows would never contain stained glass pictures, and crosses would be banned. In fact, we might ban television and movies, pictures in magazines, and photographs of our families. Since we're surrounded by "graven images" on billboards and advertising and the Internet, all of which have to do with the world, why would we stop with an icon that inspires our love for God?

During the eighth century, fundamentalist Byzantines called iconoclasts broke into churches and homes, destroying precious gold-covered icons or using the wood as steps or house shingles. Most were never recovered. The iconoclasts were finally stopped on the first Sunday of Lent in 843, in the city of Constantinople, a day that is still remembered as the Victory of Orthodoxy. After almost a hundred years of persecution directed against worship with holy icons, the Church finally proclaimed that praying with icons was favored by God.

But the iconoclasts were back in a different guise a few hundred years later. The 2003 movie *Luther* shows what can happen when zeal overcomes good sense: peasants and clergy, excited by the Reformation, raided churches and cemeteries, destroying any cross symbol on a grave or altar, burning down churches, breaking stained-glass windows, and even murdering priests, all in the guise of destroying "graven images," relics, and written indulgences.

The Church's Prescriptions

The church in the West is actually directed at *auditory* learners, with the hope that the faithful will lose themselves in listening to sermons, or hearing and replying to the phrases of worship services. The model for more charismatic or Pentecostal worship is *kinetic,* where the entire body is directed into sacred action—singing, clapping, dancing, and shouting. But the Greek, Russian, or other Orthodox sects depend on *sight* as a teaching tool. Since in its earliest years the church was populated by people who didn't know how to read, at least at more than a rudimentary level. So to help them remember the stories of the Bible, by 300 C.E., priests and their helpers began to "write" icons.[2]

According to legend, the first icon was made when King Abgar of Osroene, dying of leprosy, sent a message begging Jesus to visit him in Edessa and cure his disease. Hurrying toward Jerusalem and his crucifixion, Christ instead sent a healing gift: the imprint of his face on a cloth. The icon, known as the Mandelyon, remained in Edessa until the tenth century, when it was brought to Constantinople.[3] After the city was raided by the Crusaders in 1204, the cloth disappeared, but a number of paintings were claimed to be exact copies.

Orthodox believers seek the presence of the saint or of Jesus while gazing at icons. Many times, the painting is covered with a lacy overlay of gold or silver, as in a little icon I bought in Athens. In such icons, only the painted eyes of Mary or St. Sebastian or Jesus show through the metallic overlay, so that you gaze directly at the saint, hoping that somehow he or she is offering you grace, while the fuller glory of the painting is hidden, just as humanity's magnificent spirit lies hidden beneath a miraculous veil of flesh. And irrespective of which saint or scene the icon depicts, God is the ultimate object of contemplation and worship. The saint who is present (or actually, the aspect of God that the icon's saint models) hovers around you to remind you that Yahweh is One, Three in One.

In Greece and parts of Russia, almost every home has a prayer corner with icons. When people's minds are distracted by the cares of life, the duties and concerns of every day and the noise of the world, they can withdraw into this peaceful corner, lighting a candle or an oil-lamp in front of the icons and burning some incense. They can pray the Jesus Prayer[4] until the "soul comes to stillness and the heart tastes the sweetness of the presence of God."

Although ancient icons can cost thousands, you need not buy one of those to get started. You can get a Dover book of icons or an *Icone* calendar fairly cheaply. But my favorite vehicle to get started is Henri Nouwen's book, *Behold the Beauty of the Lord.*[5] The book contains Nouwen's personal revelation about learning to meditate with icons, and reproductions of his four favorites: Rublev's *The Old Testament Trinity, The Virgin of Vladimir, The Savior of Zvenigorod* (a portrait of Jesus that was once part of a triptych and later the underside of a wooden step!), and *The Descent of the Holy Spirit.*

Nouwen was a Roman Catholic priest from the Netherlands, as well as a psychologist, teacher, and writer of thirty books on prayer and spirituality. He discovered icon meditation when he went on a retreat at l'Arche, a religious community for people who are developmentally disabled and the friends who live with them.[6] The retreat director had laid an icon of Anton Rublev's *Old Testament Trinity* on his table. Each year following, a different icon appeared on the table in his retreat room. Nouwen ends his acknowledgments to the icon book saying, "Finally, I want to say 'Thank you' to all those who have opened my eyes as gateways to the divine. They are the many women and men in the East and the West who have come to 'behold the beauty of the Lord' (Psalm 27) by praying with icons. May this book be an encouragement to join them in this prayer."

You can also find copies of icons on the small "holy cards" in Catholic bookstores for about a quarter or less.

During the Orthodox liturgy, which lasts for hours, the priests and deacons may set icons before the people, allowing the essential Christian message of revelation to stream into their hearts. Just as Jesus became the visible image of the invisible God, so the Orthodox Christian believes that God's image is present in its full mystery in the icon. In the icon of Jesus, one can actually encounter Jesus himself. This experience is so intense that the use of icons as pictures for prayer has in recent years spread widely throughout Roman Catholic and Protestant religious communities.

Other Art for Prayer

Looking at art as prayer is certainly not restricted to icon gazing. In fact, one famous altarpiece was once used to heal a disease. During the Middle Ages, a disease commonly called St. Anthony's Fire raged through Europe. In the year 933 C.E., forty thousand people in Germany died of it and thousands more were left disfigured and crippled. During rainy winters when poor people had to scrape food from the bottom of the grain barrel, ergot, a fungus, had formed on the rye. In a wet year, the mold even appeared in the farmers' fields. And the fungus poisoned the people and caused a terrible disease.

Ergotism causes people's skin to turn red and scabby, and their arms and legs to become misshapen. People suffering from St. Anthony's Fire also had violent spasms, and seizures, and sometimes they had to get up and shake their limbs to stop the muscle contractions. St. Anthony's Fire was at first blamed on the bite of the tarantula, and the so-called "dance of agony" gave rise to a dance we know as a tarantella.

One of the hospices that treated victims of St. Anthony's Fire was at Isenheim, Germany. When victims of the disease came to the hospice, the nuns led them to the high altar of the church, where they spent an hour gazing at the altarpiece painted by Matthai Grunewald. That was the first stage of their healing: to know the possibility of participating in a miracle. The crucified Christ hangs on the cross at an extreme angle, his limbs misshapen and face covered in red scabs. In fact, all the people in the painting—John the Baptist, John the Divine, Christ's mother, and Mary Magdalene—show symptoms of St. Anthony's Fire. Because Christ suffered, Grunewald says in his altarpiece, you can be healed. And at the Isenheim hospice, thousands *were* healed. The patients knew what St. Anselm had said a few centuries earlier, "He became what we were so that we might become what he is." Knowing that Jesus Christ suffered their terrible disorder made a difference in the patients' perception of God's love and their own illness.

Only after treatment did a patient see the final "back page" of the giant altarpiece—a depiction of the Resurrection and Ascension. Here, Jesus has risen and hovers over the empty tomb and the sleeping soldiers, surrounded by a rainbow halo, which victims of the dis-

ease saw around lights (as do people with cataracts and glaucoma).
One notable element in the six paintings that make up both sides of
the triptych is the swaddling cloth, which Mary holds around Jesus in
the stable and which appears in the triptych again as the tattered,
dirty loincloth Jesus wears in the crucifixion. At the Resurrection, the
cloth, now shining white, is elevated beneath Jesus' feet.

Paintings don't usually cause miracles, even though some were
recorded at Isenheim. Besides showing patients the paintings, the
nurses at the hospice treated them with diet, poultices, heat, and such
medicines as they had. If the disease was too advanced in a patient for
a cure, his or her soul was at least healed and comforted by knowing
that Jesus endured their suffering, too. As he still does.

Jewels for a Crown

I once fell in love with an art book called *Jewels for a Crown: The Story
of the Chagall Windows.*[7] I memorized the face of every person or goat
or chicken in the pictures, which depict the twelve sons of Jacob, the
patriarchs of the twelve tribes of Israel. Chagall's assistant, Charles
Marq, developed a special process of veneering pigment on glass
which allowed Chagall to use as many as three colors on a single
uninterrupted pane, rather than being confined to the traditional
technique of separating each color pane by lean strips of lead.

Thirty years later, my husband and I visited the synagogue in the
Hadassah hospital to see the windows. Entering the quiet space, we
covered our heads and washed our hands—I thanked God for my
baptism—then stepped down on the stone floor and were surrounded by color.

The eleven-foot windows are above the rounded walls. Nobody
else was there, so we sat on the floor and gazed upward, not talking,
not analyzing, just breathing in the colors and shapes. Once in a
while, one of us said, "Look at that!" or "Oh!" but mostly we soaked
in God and God's action in history. I might be there still—might
have converted and become like Anna, who stayed in the temple all
of her eighty years—but we got terribly hungry and had to go back
to our hotel to eat.

Contemplation with icons is only one way to use art as a vehicle
for spiritual growth. Whether a painting or sculpture or photograph

is the center of your meditation, bringing Christ into the middle of the experience makes it more than seeing. Meister Eckhardt said, "The eye by which I see God is the eye with which God sees me"; when you worship with your eyes, you have called upon God to raise you toward heaven.[8]

Getting Started

Be alone, in a room where you can't hear household sounds, or the TV or music. Try to shut out the world for a little while. Instead of fragmentation, look into yourself and find quiet, unity, and a center of concentration. Then ask God to make you receptive: icon meditation is an act of receiving. Light a candle, not only to show your intention in prayer, but also because the colors and contrasts of icons reveal themselves best in candlelight. And finally, take up the picture, or lay it on a table, and look at it for about five minutes. Don't analyze it; don't analyze yourself. If your mind wanders, gently bring it back.

Teachers of icon meditation tell us to wait for a place in the icon to be "assigned" to you and let yourself be drawn into it. Every part of the icon—Christ's upraised fingers, say, or the red of Mary's veil, or the haloes around the saints—are said to have meaning and presence, and God will choose a spot to draw you into the whole of the prayer picture, or what the German theologian Karin Johne called "the function of proclamation."[9]

Taking Rublev's *Old Testament Trinity* as an icon for prayer, I am always drawn first to the dark doorways of the distant buildings. The picture isn't historically accurate—Abraham after all lived in a tent, not a two-story house with a red-tile roof, when he received three visitors and brought them a meal. But still the doorways are black and summoning: "Come inside," they say, echoing Jesus' words, "Come and see." Once I felt God drawing me into the doorways, I discovered the presence of the Trinity not only in the picture but inside me.

Certain symbols are traditional in iconography: for instance, in scenes with the Madonna and Child, the soles of the Babe's feet are usually not exposed; when they are, they symbolize his vulnerability to the world, and telegraph his future sacrifice.

Use the same method for other art if you can take the pictures or icons with you. You can buy postcards in museums or church gift shops, or find what catches your eye in a magazine. Otherwise, you'll need to make your prayer-gazing in museums or libraries, and those prayers may have to be faster. If you can find a bench or seat in a museum gallery, sit down and gaze at whatever is in front of you as prayer. Subject matter is important but not always critical—because just as everything on earth is holy, so you can project the sacred into the art you use as a centering point.

A Prayer for Gazing

God of all light and glory, teach me the silence and worship necessary to knowing you through art or icons. I beg you to be present to me, O God, and bless my gazing, which is really a search for you. Amen

CHAPTER NINE

Making Art, Doing Prayer

You have an abundance of workers: stonecutters, masons, carpenters, and all kinds of artisans without number, skilled in working gold, silver, bronze, and iron. Now begin the work, and the Lord be with you.—1 Chronicles 22:15–16

When my daughter was about two and a half, I took her to an "art in the park" event where artists were at their easels or creating sculpture of all kinds. We stopped to watch one talented woman who was working on a luminous, almost magical painting of a coat thrown over a chair. My little girl watched for a few moments as the woman laid layer after layer of color and wax medium on the picture; then the child could stand no more. She rushed up to the painter and cried, "Me draw! Me draw!"

And to tell the truth, *I* wanted to paint, too, as I watched that artist. Sometimes just seeing fine art can make you want to do it yourself, whether you're planning an eight-foot marble sculpture on the same level with Michelangelo's *David,* or a finger-painting to hang on the refrigerator. When you long to create something visual and tangible, I think that impulse comes straight from the Holy Spirit, who fills us with life and expectation and invention. Art doesn't require expensive materials or a background in painting or sculpture. Art as prayer demands only two things: intention, of course, and the belief that God gives you the ability to create.

Creativity is a form of the spiritual energy that propels our lives, and you can capture that energy to create art, or make a Peruvian pepper soufflé, or sing in the church choir. You have more of that energy than you imagine: if you acknowledge that creativity comes from God, you'll never run out.

When I was the art teacher in a Christian parish school, one of my favorite exercises was to bring the kids in and tell them they had to be silent while they made things. Each student had several kinds of paper and a little sack of equipment: crayons, cut-up pieces of screen, blotters, colored tissue paper, glue, scissors, wallpaper scraps, fabric and whatever else popped into my mind as I was filling sacks.

I always explained to them that God had seeded them with creativity, an energy that they could use to play a game or learn math or draw pictures—or talk. In these exercises, we tried to pour *all* that energy into creating art. I usually wrote a couple of subjects on the blackboard, asking them to make a picture of a loud noise, a happy day, or a dream.

I was always gratified at the creativity those kids expressed. One boy who was so dyslexic he was hardly functioning suddenly blossomed as an abstract artist with a real flair for composition and color, and a girl whose school papers were usually almost encyclopedic created with torn tissue an abstract design for stained glass.

You maybe expending creative energy in other ways—probably in some worthy activity. But since God's gifts are unlimited, try to direct some of that creativity into art-as-prayer, in which both you and God can delight.

Not everyone can become a master painter, but since pictures are only one aspect of doing prayer as art, you have scores of other opportunities. If you *do* want to create drawings or paintings, experiment awhile to find the medium where you feel most comfortable. Feel free to create either abstract paintings or pictures of people and things. I have one artistic friend who journals in exquisite calligraphy and then faces each page with a watercolor flower. Those of us who like to paint or draw don't have to be that facile; we can "play as prayer," perhaps creating pictures of things we love best as offerings to God.

A generation ago, Marshall McLuhan wrote a book called *The Medium is the Massage,* in which he says that people adapt to their environment through a certain balance or ratio of their senses, and the primary medium of the age brings out a particular sense ratio. McLuhan sees every medium as an extension of some human faculty, with the media of communication thus exaggerating this or that particular sense. McLuhan said that all human invention is based on our bodies, including our limbs and nerves.[1] To his words I want to add that art is an extension of the spirit, and creating art can be a direct line to heaven, a response to an environment in which God is always present.

If you rouse your creativity, you'll find your medium, whether it's making sculptures from found objects or taking pictures or painting portraits in the classical Flemish style. Some of the "doing art" occupations you might try or renew or continue are photography, metal sculpture, clay modeling, or "junk" art (beauty created from found objects, scrap metal, cardboard, machine parts, etc.). I have a friend who fingerpaints with oil paints in cookie sheets, then "monoprints" one copy by carefully pressing parchment onto the creation. His prints are now in some demand in his community; he says he's "just playing," which is a lot like just praying.

Photography

I love to take pictures for two reasons. First of all, I'm not terribly mechanical, so I can't think about myself much when I'm trying to remember how to set my camera at f-16 and a hundredth of a second. And I get pretty involved with my subject. I wouldn't lie on wet grass to read, as much as I love reading; but to immortalize the lavender underside of a hedgehog mushroom in the woods, I'd probably throw myself down in a swamp. I can't show off or even be self-aware when I'm photographing anything.

My most spiritually inspired pictures aren't the wildflowers I love to photograph, but black-and-white shots of inanimate objects: a chipped iron bedstead in the corner of a garden, three white eggs on a cherrywood table, a little Japanese stone lantern in a bed of round rocks. I feel prayerful when I shoot this kind of subject because through these things, God shows me glimpses of perfection and lets me find beauty in the ordinary. Because the setups are simple, I don't have to look for obscure meanings. Three white eggs have their own God-given beauty. The iron bedstead connects what is fabricated to what is natural in the garden. And almost any kind of Asian stone structure has the look of a temple.

But you don't have to invest thousands in a camera to use photography as prayer. Just buy one of those "throwaway" or one-use cameras and head outside or downtown, accompanied by—as usual—intention! If you're taking pictures for God, you'll find the right subjects and you won't have to struggle with that pesky technical stuff until you're ready to branch out.

Photography is more than recording scenes. The main equipment for good photography, the kind you could call prayerful, is the eye. Only you can see things a particular way; capturing that seeing is the trick. Even a snapshot can have your particular view, your individual concept of reality.

Clay as Meditation

One of my favorite worship choruses is "Abba, Father," in which we sing that we are clay and God the potter. The song of course echoes Isaiah 64:8, which says, "Yet, O Lord, you are our Father; we are the clay, and you are our potter; we are all the work of your hand."

And it turns out that we may *really* be God's clay. Recent scientific studies suggest that life may have indeed sprung from clay, just as both the Bible and the Qur'an proclaim. A team at the Howard Hughes Medical Institute and Massachusetts General Hospital in Boston said they had shown that materials in clay support processes similar to those that may have given rise to life. The ongoing study is very technical, but the gist is that a clay mixture called *montmorillonite* not only helps form little bags of fat and liquid but helps cells use genetic material called RNA. That, in turn, is one of the key processes of life.[2]

So now, since God made you of clay *and* in God's own image, seek both those roots within yourself. Get into the clay.

Sit for a few minutes with a ball of thrown clay[3] in your hands while you center yourself for prayer. Don't squeeze the ball, but just let your hands warm it while you center yourself for prayer. After you feel yourself relaxed and able to work with the clay begin to mold it without keeping shape in mind. In fact, many people like to close their eyes.

If you think you're being pulled in more than one direction, work the clay out in several places. If life is squeezing you, push one area into the center. Make a shape somewhere else that symbolizes happy experiences. And so on. Then let your clay prayer dry so you can keep it on desk or dresser to remind you that God is the potter and you are the clay.

If you enjoy actually modeling forms with clay, choose a subject you'll enjoy looking at (or giving away as a special gift). If you plan to fire your sculpture, be sure to create a hollow space inside. I've made some small terra-cotta sculptures with crumpled aluminum foil as an armature, or center-holder. But don't get so caught up in the technicalities of the medium that you forget you're doing it for God. And with God.

A Holy Space for Living

Since you spend a lot more time in your house than you do at church, home should be your first, basic worship space. You may have a small altar or prayer corner, but your whole house is a sacred space, where you live and pray and think and create. So "interior decorating" becomes a spiritual process where you create areas that shimmer with what's holy.

Feng shui was once a little-known Asian practice in which the furniture and other objects of a house are arranged and rearranged to let the "chi," or sacred energy, flow through to benefit the people who live there. Nowadays, you can see feng shui practiced on TV's *Trading Spaces* or *Clean Sweep*. Whether you want to use all the esoteric principles or just work with the basic idea of making your environment beautiful and sacred is an important spiritual exercise because you're celebrating your life. Your surroundings have a powerful impact on your prayers—and vice versa. Some people like a fairly austere, Zen-style home, with faded wood floors, simple furnishings, and as much open space as possible. Others prefer a Louis XIV environment with rococo picture frames, white and gold everywhere, and rich fabrics. Most of us have homes somewhere in the middle, with piles of mail that need sorting, maybe some dishes on the sink, and an amalgam of furniture in several styles. No matter what your situation, create an environment that reflects your tastes *and* glorifies God.

Wait: before you rush out to buy a matched set of crucifixes or a prie-dieu for the living room, think about what really glorifies the Creator. Psalm 29:2 in the King James Version says, "Give unto the Lord the glory due unto his name; worship the Lord in the beauty of holiness." Did you catch that word "beauty"? That doesn't mean ornate or expensive; it means creating a home that welcomes others and pleases the vision of its inhabitants. And I think getting rid of mess and clutter is one of the finest ways to pray (except maybe in my home office, where, on some days, I can't even find the phone).

It took me nine years to make my house right—I don't have a lot of time for decorating and this was a brand-new house that didn't need re-doing yet. I knew for years that something wasn't working, but until we finally replaced our carpet with laminated hardwood flooring, painted the back dining room wall red, and hung some downright improbable curtains, I never really enjoyed the place as I do now. And I think I did a kind of unconscious "feng shui" for arrangement balance. I have some books on the subject and though I don't subscribe to the Chinese—or any other kind of—astrology or feng shui tarot, I do think the idea of letting *spiritual* power, which Asians call *qi* or *chi,* flow through space is a universal wisdom. Clutter is distracting to a state of prayer and big pieces of furniture that block that energy flow as well as vision aren't felicitous for a sense of balance.

Decorating can be expensive. Maybe right now you can just shove some furniture around and buy fresh flowers until you can afford to paint or buy new pieces. So clean up messes, organize books and files, hang those pictures that are on the guest room bed and remember that you're praying while you push that heavy dresser and create beauty in your home.

Flowers and *Ikebana*

Ikebana, or Japanese flower arrangement, has been practiced for a long time. The Ikebana Sangetsu school was founded on the teachings of Mokichi Okada, an early twentieth-century healer. He believed that the creation of paradise on earth, where truth, beauty, and virtue prevailed, was mandatory for the preservation of humanity. Okada filled his home and work centers with the flower arrangements and calligraphy on parchment that he created every day. He also designed gardens as "sacred grounds for all the world's exhausted ones," parks still found today in the Japanese cities of Hakone, Atami, and Kyoto.

Okada's flower compositions follow some basic principles: he never forced flowers or branches into a shape; he chose flowers that reflected the seasons; to preserve their life force, he ordered them quickly after cutting; he grouped flowers as if painting a picture; and he arranged them with joy, aware of transmitting joy and healing to others. He wanted to see arrangements in homes, schools, and businesses and prison cells to elevate consciousness.

If you want to arrange flowers as a form of prayer, you might start with something like a few Dutch iris in a low container. Or pick nasturtiums and arrange them with dried gray leaves in a pottery bowl. Or if you're experienced, buy some beautiful blossoms and make an arrangement with uneven numbers and heights, with a base as wide as the flowers' height. Think of some quality, such as peace or healing or joy that you want to transmit to anyone who sees your arrangement (including yourself).

One noted flower designer, Anthony Ward, creates daily floral offerings for the Dalai Lama. Ward loves to include sunflowers: "For his smile," says Ward, "and the color of his robes."[4]

Working with real plants brings a spiritual quality to what you do with them. The fragrances not only of flowers but of the leaves, or of the stems when you cut them, permeate your sense of smell. You can hear the rustling of blossoms and greenery as they brush against each other. Your need to touch bursts with energy as you arrange and rearrange, and at the end, you have a visual feast, an arranged prayer.

But you can use the same principles of *ikebana* or other prayerful arranging with dried or perhaps silk materials. Even the most arcane volumes on feng shui tell us that if you can't have growing plants in a room, at least add some artificial ones. Many restaurants nowadays know that green plants create a serene atmosphere, and those eateries that can't manage live philodendrons and ivy have pots of some that look real. One of my favorite downtown coffee shops has huge hanging baskets of what I really believed were real impatiens and fuschias, until the day I reached up to touch their silk surfaces. Those arrangements add gaiety and color to what would otherwise be an ordinary "waffle shop."

From Junk to Joy

My friend Marianne makes art out of nothing. She saves her junk mail and in a painstaking process, creates handmade stationery and picture matting in various colors, sometimes sprinkled with glitter or tiny stars or red ladybugs. She grinds paper and water in her food processor, strains it several times to remove some of the liquid, adds liquid starch or white glue and decorative elements like sequins, autumn leaves or bark, and sprays of cinnamon and turmeric, then spreads the pulp onto framed screens with weighted covers. She makes it look easy, but I've tried it several times and have never developed her proficiency. I *did*, however, make some thick sheets I glued onto notebook covers, then kept the notebooks as journals. And if you're willing to experiment and spend time spreading, drying, "couching" (stacking the sheets together), you, too, can be a paper-maker. I would suggest that you find a book on handmade paper at your library or bookstore.

Her other art expression starts with collecting real rubbish. She pulls over on the freeway to pick up shreds from tires or tailpipes. She tramps through vacant lots and recycling centers, and even visits landfills for scrap metal and odd knobs, nails, and broken jewelry and odd hardware.

Then she either welds or hot-glues her findings onto thin plywood in cross shapes, moving the cabachon from a broken necklace here and placing a cluster of rusty nails there. At first her compositions look like disorganized trash, but suddenly they take on glory. Her junk-art crosses have such a quality of holiness and purpose that churches have bought her largest ones for chapels and parish halls. Her exquisite sense of design, and her ability to see the divine in what someone has thrown away, remind us that Jesus Christ is the stone the builders rejected. You don't have to have an overwhelming talent to create beautiful junk assemblages. You *do* need some patience, because the processes require time and persistence. Want to try? Take a walk through some vacant lots to see what you can find. Then get out your glue gun and start to work.

Textile Art as Prayer

Textiles offer so many ways to create art, and art as prayer, that even someone who doesn't feel very creative can sew or weave or tie-dye. I have seen some amazing tie-dyed or batik wall hangings that convey a sacred quality. A friend who lives in a tall glass house in the California redwoods has a fifteen-foot square of tie-dyed peach silk in his entry, one that looks like a colorful summer sunrise. Just stepping into that house makes me feel reverent. Although we rarely wear tie-dyed T-shirts any more, artful examples are turning up in galleries all over the country.

Batik uses wax to mask certain areas of fabric before each dip into high-powered dyes. The process has many steps, but you can start by painting with warm liquid beeswax (or a mixture of beeswax and paraffin) a simple design, such as a spiral or a Celtic cross, on a square unbleached muslin. While the design dries, make a hot potful of dye, following the instructions on the package. Dip the fabric in, then spread it on a towel or cutting board to dry again. If you want another color, use wax to mask off areas of the first color, then dip again.

When you plunge the wax-treated fabric into hot dye, some of the painting cracks and allows tiny bits of dye to seep in, creating that unmistakable batik character. Making batik is a lot more tedious than painting a picture, so it has longer opportunities to become prayer.

You might like to place a big piece of burlap on a frame, and hook or punch a rug. Or make a small loom by pounding nails at even intervals into a wood frame, then warping it with vertical string or yarn, and using a big needle as a bobbin. Weaving that way or on a big professional loom can teach you a lot about God. Even though your woven fabric looks beautiful, the underside can be messy, with hanging strings and knotted threads. I like to remember that when my life or someone else's looks out-of-kilter, I can learn in my weaving prayer that a messy life is just the underside of something God's weaving.

A Prayer for Making Art

Dear God, you are the greatest artist of all, and you have splashed the earth with color and movement. Let your artistry flow through me so that I can pray with my hands. Amen

CHAPTER TEN

Hands in the Earth: The Prayer of Planting

Awake, O north wind, and come, O south wind! Blow upon my garden that its fragrance may be wafted abroad. Let my beloved come to his garden, and eat its choicest fruits.—**Song of Solomon 4:16**

Hildegard of Bingen's illuminations have brought real excitement into my spiritual life, and at retreats I love to show slides of them and talk about their meaning. One of her paintings shows Satan and his angels as bright gold stars falling from heaven, turning dark and finally black in the soil and at last sinking down into a kind of white permafrost. Hell is a cold place. But even as they die, some sparks lie in the dark soil. God never wastes anything: the power of the fallen angels now belongs to humanity, and Hildegard thought it might lie in the earth. It does, of course: the atoms of minerals that were born in the stars, like uranium and carbon and nitrogen, are dancing with power, and Hildegard wrote better than she knew.

But I think we also touch *spiritual* power when we have our hands and minds in the soil. We're surrounded not only by angels and clouds of witnesses: spiritual energy abounds within us and without.

There's a reason why your heart skips when you look at a blossoming cherry tree or the way a pinkish boulder on a hillside complements nearby rust-colored dockweed. God created a planet with enough beauty and whimsy to make you suck in your breath a hundred times a day if, as a Buddhist would put it, you're looking mindfully.

And if you go outside and putter in your yard, vegetable patch, or community garden for a day, pinching this and transplanting that, you'll take a deep breath and let the scents of mown grass or sweet peas fill your lungs; and as you exhale, you might smile your joy at being on God's planet.

I don't know how you define "soul," but every plant in my house and yard has *presence,* and communicates its pleasure or terror or depression. I've seen squash vines that look perky until the flowers change into zucchini: then I witness the drama of childbirth, with the vines pouring their all into their "children," neglecting their own welfare. But when brussels sprouts send up the stalk that will bear the tiny cabbages, they are at their green best, and you can almost hear them proclaim their pride.

Nothing can express the need for water more dramatically than a piggyback plant, or *tolmeia,* when it's thirsty. One of the most-grown houseplants, it grows wild in my nearby woods. It hurls itself downward, its leaves upside down on the table or soil. The whole picture fills gardeners with guilt and sends them to get the watering can. On the other hand, my Christmas cactus, which actually blooms around Easter, is stalwart and polite. If I go out of town and my husband forgets to water it, the brave little succulent just stands still, not growing but not withering either.

Plants have no soul? Then who is in those leaves and stems and blossoms, telling me their stories? If God is speaking through the piggyback and the cactus and the fast-growing poplar saplings in my backyard, then they are in God and they therefore have souls. Buddhist writer Pamela Bloom wrote in *Spirituality and Health,* "Where flowers differ from paint or clay . . . is that they have *prana*—life force—something you can actually feel with your body as you handle floral elements with a new sensitivity."[1]

When people come to me for spiritual direction, I always suggest that they grow something, anything: an acre of corn, a potted cyclamen plant, or something in between. When you go outdoors to pull weeds, be sure to declare that an action of prayer, and regard the soil as sacred. When you sink your fingers into dirt, you're connecting to creation, no matter how much soil you're working with. Someone said every farmer is a mystic, and whoever said it was right. You get sense of the miraculous, first from planting seeds or bulbs or corms or eyes, and then seeing the soil break with tiny sprouts that become plants and finally flowers or fruit or both.

If you have no yard, or if physical limitations keep you inside, start a little indoor farm. One pot of ivy or philodendron will not only add some attractive greenery to your environment, it will let you start being a partner in creation. Four or five plants, maybe including something rare and lovely like an orchid or blooming epiphyllium cactus, can draw you closer to God and your own inner spirit. Growing is a holy occupation, one everyone should try.

Planting Seeds

I remember that when I was a child, I felt amazed that a seed knew how to become grass or morning glories or tomatoes. Didn't they ever get confused? Was it possible to buy marigold seeds, with pictures of the flowers glowing all orange and yellow on the packet, and find out that one of the marigold seeds forgot its identity and turned into a white lily?

No, my parents and grandmothers and teachers told me, but I kept watching. I pointed out that two of the eggs our hen had set on turned out to be ducks, and my mother said that was on purpose. Whose purpose? The hen's or the ducks'? Ours, my mother said, and I was still awed and confused. But sure enough, unless I dropped a stray aster seed into the marigolds, what we planted was what we got. And after that, all our eggs hatched into baby chickens with bright black eyes and yellow down.

What the story of the seed says is that you can trust God. Trust and faith are the two most important elements in planting. Trust that an olive tree will not bear apples or hazelnuts, that God has installed some kind of order even in randomness, and that you are safe from disaster when you plant.

Faith is planting a tree that may not bear fruit in your lifetime. And it's believing in the sacredness of the dirt, the earth, that the sanctity and holiness of life dance in every atom of soil and vegetation. God gave us trees for oxygen and shade and beauty, flowers for joy and innocence, and the sweet figs that grow on my front-yard tree for moments of absolute delight.

A joke making the rounds tells about a silly woman who kept praying to win the lottery. Day after day, she begged God to let her win, but she never did. When she complained, God said, "Honey, work with me. Buy a ticket." Well, the same thing is true about gardening. Prayer, faith, and trust won't overcome poor soil or too much rain or hot summer days that can damage tender plants. You've got to work with God and make a little compost, sprinkle some water, and pull those weeds.

Vine and Branches

"Abide in me as I abide in you," Jesus told the disciples. If you really want to understand Jesus' words in the amazing fifteenth chapter of John *and* use planting as prayer, grow grapes. Since nearly everyone who had a southern slope in Palestine also had a vineyard, wine-centered terms were undoubtedly familiar to the disciples who had their feet washed at that Last Supper.

You can get bare root vines at home and garden stores in the late winter or early spring. Grapes need a lot of sunlight and high temperatures to ripen, so plant them on the south or southwest side of your yard, using a wire frame or fence to hold them in place. Grape vines, like olive trees, are always deemed sacred by every religion, so whether you're mindful or not, you perform a holy task when you thrust a grapevine into the soil.

As cool autumn weather moves in, you'll begin to see what Jesus was talking about when he said, "Just as the branch cannot bear fruit by itself unless it abides in the vine, neither can you unless you abide in me." The next year's grapes will only grow on new shoots, so every autumn the grower has to prune off a whole summer's tangled shoots, vines and leaves. The vinegrower reduces the vine back to a brown, dry T-shape—a main stem and two very short shoots coming from the top. Notice this: "Whoever does not abide in me is thrown away like a branch and withers; such branches are gathered, thrown into the fire, and burned." Indeed, you *should* dispose of all the pruned-off vines in case they have diseases or bug infestations that could linger in your garden. But what about "abide"? How does that have anything to do with grapes?

The DNA and shoot formation lie within the pruned-off "tee." Even in ancient times, growers believed the new growth was waiting within the vine stem. It *abides* in that trunk, waiting for the warmth of spring to bring up the sap and send the shoots and branches out onto the wire frame. They are contained within the vine, or stem, and by abiding there through the winter, they will be ready for a late summer crop of firm, juicy grapes. Just like those of us who keep Jesus' commands.

Creatures Great and Small

My friend lived in an impressive home with the wild Willamette River making a fence for her backyard. She had planted a pear tree and finally, after several years' growth, fruit had formed. Big D'Anjou pears hung off the limbs like temple bells, and she went to bed one Wednesday, planning to pick her first crop in the morning.

But during that night, beavers climbed out of the river. They chewed the tree down, then ate all the pears and left. My friend walked out at dawn to find that her precious pear tree had been chopped down and the crop had been stolen. (To add insult to injury, the beavers came back the next night and took the tree itself into the river to form part of a dam.) Of course my friend didn't have very warm feelings about beavers and threatened to annihilate every one she saw. In fact, she wanted to declare all the beavers in the river guilty, and hang each one of them. Fortunately for the beavers, she got got busy with something else and their lives were spared.

At my house, the enemies are slugs. Lane County, Oregon probably holds the world's record for the number of slugs per square foot. At the annual Eugene celebration, the main float in the parade features a Slug Queen, who usually wears a tight, shiny gown, often with green and yellow sequins; she and her court all have long strips of clear plastic wrap fastened to the back bottoms of their dresses, to look like slug or snail trails.

One warm summer night I picked more than a hundred slugs off *one* ten-foot row of sugar snap peas. I tried putting out beer, and they

got sleek and fat on it. I don't like using eggshells that cut them to rib-
bons. And I don't have time to pick slugs every night. Maybe I should
just try mechanical answers, such as plastic barriers. Or let the slugs
have their share of my garden. Or hire a gardener who will poison
them without telling me. Whatever your garden pests are—crows or
blue jays that eat your cherries, snails or slugs that shear off your lettuce or eat the roses, or red spiders that damage the fuschias—should
you poison or otherwise kill them? Especially when you have planted
as prayer?

The Dalai Lama would say no. Buddhists do not poison thrips or
cucumber beetles or ants or aphids, and the Dalai Lama, like Albert
Schweitzer, would tell us that if we cannot help a species, we should at
least vow not to harm it. Especially if we're gardening as a form of
devotion to God.

That puts your faith on its mettle. Are you going to put out snail
bait or spray pesticide on your rhododendrons, or let everything eat
your garden at will? Or, so long as your precautions are "organic," is it
all right to poison your pests?

Nasturtiums and marigolds of course ward off some creatures, but
they don't do it all. I always brag that I'm a sort of Buddhist-minded
Episcopalian until varmints attack my garden, which I have planted as
a form of prayer. Then any compassionate leanings disappear. For the
sake of my own lungs I don't spray dangerous substances or lace my
soil with relatives of the dangerous herbicide 2,4-D But I do put out
slug bait that's harmless to birds, and I occasionally spray with insec-
ticide soap.

When I was a little girl, my father planted a garden and fenced it;
but then he planted a "rabbit garden" outside the fence. Lettuce,
tomatoes, cabbages and berries, all for the pleasure of whatever little
animals lived near our Arizona high-desert home. "There's enough to
go around," he always said, and sure enough, neither rabbits nor kan-
garoo rats ever burrowed under our garden fence to attack the crop,
and our local donkeys, who were allowed to wander wild and who ate
everything from prickly-pear cactus to newspaper, especially enjoyed
the orange and grapefruit skins we also threw into the rabbit area.

What all that means is that I don't just compost and import
worms and ladybugs and praying mantises to control pests: I also
grow some flowers that slugs may eat in a corner of the yard. I let

them lunch on the back side of my big snowball tree, and they may nibble the rhubarb leaves that I wouldn't cook anyway because the leaves' oxalic acid is dangerous. And I throw inferior cobs of corn into the blackberries at the top of our slope, because that bramble is full of bird habitat. There really is enough to go around, so part of my outdoor prayer is nourishing other creatures. I have to confess, however, that the occasional rattlesnake that travels into our yard meets his death at our hands. As the man facing an enemy with a battle-axe said, you can carry love too far.

Getting Started

Begin in a small way: planning a major landscaping could become less a prayer and more a project. In an indoor pot or a flower bed outside, plant a seed or two (you might like to start an outside plant, like a tomato, indoors until the soil warms up). Bless the seed, and bless the dirt that covers it; then holding the pot in your hands, or with your hands on the dirt outside where you planted it, offer the plant and soil to God. I make no guarantees that the plant will thrive, but it can't hurt, can it?

A Prayer for Gardening

Creator of all nature, bless me as I share the process with you. Amen

CHAPTER ELEVEN

Hearth Prayers

On that day . . . the cooking pots in the house of the Lord shall be as holy as the bowls in front of the altar. —Zechariah 14:20

Few of us cook over an open fire, unless we're camping or toasting marshmallows at a picnic. But when I visited the pre-Revolution home of my great-great-great-great-grandparents, where the floors, walls, bricks, and windows are the originals, I saw the black iron crane in the fireplace where pots hung and could be swung out for stirring, and spits for turning meat. The people who now own the house swung the crane out so I could try to lift an iron pot onto it. Women had to be strong in those days; my wrist couldn't raise it.

Women rose at dawn to tend fire where the breakfast gruel simmered, and by the time they had heated enough water to wash up the dishes, they had to start a soup or stew or a roasted joint for the evening meal. A lot of prayers have undoubtedly been murmured over hearths, reaching back to the days when nomadic herders built desert fires with whatever fuel they could find. At least *some* of those prayers had to be pleas for enough strength to go on, and even those who didn't petition God prayed by cooking.

In contrast, I got up this morning, opened my packet of oatmeal, and held it under my hot spigot, which serves up almost-boiling water anytime I want it. I threw beans into an electric grinder, then poured some of that same steaming water in my one-cup dripper to make a mug of fragrant Starbuck's coffee. The whole process took no more than ten minutes. But my coffee maker and hot spigot are as sacred in this house as my ancestors' pots and cranes were in theirs.

Hearth prayers aren't just those that you pray when you kindle the "fire," which in your house may be, like mine, turning on the range or plugging in an electric skillet. That doesn't always feel like a sacred act, so you may need to say some of the prayers at the end of this chapter to get started.

Sometimes we get the idea that a thing has to be "natural," or at least primitive, to be holy. Magazine soft-focus pictures that depict wooden spoons in ancient earthenware bowls, accompanied by sprigs of rosemary and vials of raspberry vinegar, look artsy, but they aren't a realistic image of the way most people live today. I can't write books if I'm looking for wild rosemary or making vinegar, and I *really* don't want to slaughter hogs or put up seven hundred quarts of tomatoes. What matters isn't how primitive your utensils are or whether you grow your wheat and grind your own flour, but the spirit you bring to cooking and housekeeping and your front porch.

My mother and grandmothers always washed their hands with soap when they entered the kitchen so I grew up doing the same thing. And when the warm water runs over my fingers and the soap lathers up between them, I think about my baptism, which didn't only wash away any babyhood sins, but made me a part of our spiritual family, the Body of Christ. I am not only grateful for my baptism, I am beholden to it. Which doesn't always suit my purposes: I'd much rather take in a movie with my husband than take some cookies and companionship over to a woman down the block, a miserable, unhappy woman who looks for things to be mad about. But my baptism calls me to go see her and treat her with patience.

The greatest benefit of my baptism, however, was being filled with the Holy Spirit, who gives me my prayers and prays them in me. At moments when I think I can't pray or when I'm too mad at God and don't want to pray, God the Holy Spirit just goes right ahead. In a few minutes I hear about an earthquake on the news and I beg God for

mercy, or my aging doggie lies down under my desk and I thank God
for the dog's years with me. The Holy Spirit not only doesn't abandon
me, but insists on keeping me in prayer.

I'm not a neat cook; my style is more intuitive. I start sticking garlic cloves into a pork roast and decide to go outside and clip some
cilantro. While I'm hovering over my herb garden to get the rosemary, I want some fresh sage, too. And when I get the roast pierced
and herbed, I think how good it would taste if I basted it with red
wine and orange juice. . . . This is adventuresome cooking, not bril-
liance. Some of my creations taste wonderful while others are edible
but nothing more.

But cooking as prayer is intentionally creating a food offering to
God. Cooking as prayer is acting out your devotion to Christ in a way
that benefits you and anyone else you're feeding. The kitchen is a holy
place. A hearth is the oldest sign of civilization, moving fire from an
accident of lightning or other natural cause into the hands of
humans. The Greek myths say the Titan Prometheus stole fire from
Zeus and gave it to the people of earth. Zeus in turn punished
Prometheus with an eagle who would forever tear the Titan's liver
out, but never grant him death: fire elevated humans to the level of
gods and goddesses.

I doubt that I could be called a kitchen goddess, but my stove and
sink and counters are sacred, and I'm grateful for whoever gave us
fire because now I don't have to chomp into a raw haunch of
mastodon for dinner or break my teeth on a wild beet, nor must I
rub two sticks or stones together to get a spark. Fire is indeed a holy
element, and cooking as prayer includes gratitude. And if you have
children at home, let a kid cook with you sometimes so they, too, can
apprehend holiness.

And what I cook over my "fire" must be holy, too. Paul and the
author of Revelation have both advised us not to eat food sacrificed
to idols,[1] and though I don't see a lot of idols around, I see a lot of
idolatry. This has thrown me into a kind of quandary: if I buy rib-eye
steaks or ground turkey from a supermarket, am I supporting the god
of greed? When I pay extra to get organic lettuce and parsnips, do I
benefit humanity or just pay off another avaricious distributor? I
don't have the facilities to raise my own beef (and after feeding a
chubby, long-lashed animal every day I couldn't eat it, anyway) and

my present home doesn't have the right soil or space to grow many vegetables. And I certainly can't raise grain and grind my own flour or rice or tapioca. So I have to re-dedicate my food to God with a quick prayer of sacrifice and a request for blessing. At first you might feel silly, waving a stalk of celery or placing your hands on a package of biscuit mix and then offering it to God, but when you do, you've restored the innocence of the food and prayed to neutralize any greed or graft connected to it for human use. Cooking as prayer needs to be artful. That doesn't mean "skillful," but means you should be as creative and focused and excited as if you were painting a picture or composing a symphony. Just think: the chocolate milk you stir up for your child will give him or her a big helping of calcium and a dollop of magnesium, both needed for strong bones and muscles. The chicken you fry for your family is the central sacrifice in a feast of love. And your Christmas ham, served to friends and guests, rejoices in the Incarnation in a tangible way.

What if you live alone? You can still create a sacrificial kitchen, even though you cook for one person. Your own body needs to be fed and cared for, and Jesus Christ is always with you as giver and guest. If you take as many pains in preparing a meal for yourself, then God will be as honored as if you held a dinner for twelve. Use the best ingredients, even if all you're making is a bologna sandwich: use fresh, crunchy lettuce, whole grain bread, and the finest mustard, and dedicate it to God. Not only will you enjoy the sandwich more, but you'll sit down with gratitude to eat in a prayerful, maybe celebratory, mood. And whenever possible, invite someone to come cook and eat with you.

Every meal you cook has the potential of being a source of merry-making or festivity. Even a funeral dinner celebrates the life of the person who has passed on, and trying to prepare a meal when the worst has happened—your child uses drugs, your spouse leaves you, or you're losing your home to foreclosure—the food you prepare can be a witness, and will declare your belief that Christ himself is involved in the solution to your problem.

Today after breakfast I wrote for three hours, and then my kitchen spiritual practice began with chestnuts. Cooking is one of the most meditative things I do. I prayed an ancient Celtic hearth prayer as I turned on the stove and sorted the chestnuts, thanking God for their beautiful smooth shells.

Julian of Norwich saw God in something like a hazelnut; I find God today in these beautiful, smooth creations. The pale winter sun danced bravely on the south walls and I praised God that we're already a month past the solstice; the sun is moving northward again and midsummer will come with chestnut blossoms and warm weather's own feasts.

I boiled and peeled the chestnuts, almost weeping over the sweet cream-colored meat as I peeled off the dark shiny outer skin. I decided to saute them and sprinkle them with brown sugar. What a feast for my eyes—the golden sugar, the dark butter, the chestnuts like pearls. Perhaps this is how God sees the human race: gleaming in the darkness, shining from the sweetness of Christ.

Chestnuts contain a score of nutrients, enhanced by the sweet ginger tea I made and drank while the nuts were cooking. Their fragrance reminds me of the day I stood at Syntagma Square, in Athens, where I watched the changing of the fierce, short-skirted army guard. I ate hot roasted chestnuts right under the trees they grow on. Chestnut flowers smell like faint lilacs, and the nuts grow inside a frilly burred husk. How various, how beautiful are the products of this planet! As I bite into my sugared treat, I almost kneel down with ecstasy. Thank God for my ability to taste . . . but greater thanks for my ability to cook. Because bringing food and herbs and salt and heat together in divine amounts is an occupation worthy of an angel.

A hearth prayer of course should include blessings and devotion for a whole house. Try dusting as a form of prayer and you'll enjoy it a lot more. Sweep the front porch as you would a temple, and once in a while, walk or dance through the whole house, letting God's blessing pervade you and your surroundings.

Getting Started

Before you begin praying through cooking or housework, you might like to learn some *said* prayers to warm you up. I like to use a variety of prayers, including those from many sources.

The following is an Omaha Indian prayer whose source is unknown:

May the house wherein I dwell be blessed;
My good thoughts here possess me;
May my path of life be straight and true;
My dreams as here I lie be joyous;
All above, below, about me
May the house I love be hallowed[2]

A Prayer for Cooking
From the Book of Common Prayer

Visit, we beseech Thee, O Lord, this dwelling, and drive far from it all snares of the enemy; let Thy holy Angels dwell herein, to preserve us in peace; and let Thy blessing be upon us forever. Through Christ our Lord. Amen

And finally, a table grace I learned at potlucks, school lunches, and dinner parties from Father Fred Fenton. He says the source is unknown.

O Thou that clothest the lilies
And feedest the birds of the air,
That bringest the lamb to the pasture
And the hart to the water's side,
Who has multiplied loaves and fishes
And converted water to wine,
Do Thou come to our table
As giver and guest to dine. Amen

CHAPTER TWELVE

Holy Food

I am the living bread that came down from heaven. Whoever eats of this bread will live forever; and the bread that I will give for the life of the world is my flesh.—John 6:51

I was scarfing down pizza as fast as I could. I'd been on three planes that day, without any lunch or dinner, and now, at almost ten o'clock at night, I was famished. My grandson watched me for a few minutes and said, chuckling, "Grandmother, you eat like a velociraptor."

"Hey, I'm hungry. I was deprived all day," I answered, pushing the last bite into my mouth. Of course, my idea of deprivation wouldn't stand up where people are really desperate for food. I'd eaten breakfast that morning, and each of the airlines had bestowed a package of pretzels on me.

We say we're starving when we want lunch, famished when dinner is an hour late, and deprived when we've had to skip a meal. But however we express it, the human desire for food is universal. We don't sleep in trees at night anymore, but we're still hunter-gatherers: instead of looking for roots and berries, we spend our days hunting money at work and we gather food in the supermarket; the process is still the same.

But Christ's Incarnation changed everything. When he is at the center of our lives, the world's system of reference goes down and is then restored within us as the Kingdom of Heaven. And one of the best ways to remember that is to make every meal an extension of the Communion table. If ours wasn't a religion that included eating and drinking, then we might find it harder to eat as prayer; but since the Eucharist is the centerpiece of our faith, since food—bread with wine—is what our religion is about, then every meal is an extension of the Lord's Supper. Consuming food becomes a sacred activity, one that combines intention, gratitude, and celebration as the main courses.

Remember those three elements: *intention,* which means you dedicate eating the meal to God's glory; *gratitude,* being in a state of thanksgiving for God's generosity and also for being able to taste and enjoy good food; and *celebration,* the mood you take to the table.

Maybe Sunday after church is the best time to put this concept into practice the first time: think of the Eucharist as the "first course" in your meal. You can go home, still tasting the wine, to find the perfect roast ready to come out of the oven where you left it cooking, or visit your favorite restaurant in a reverent mood, and order foods from an interesting menu. Even if you head for the fishing hole and stop for hot dogs, your prayerful intentions can turn them into nectar and ambrosia, or whatever it is that they eat in heaven.

Eat with a conscience. If you can eat lower on the food chain, do so to honor God's creation. Celebration of tofu or wheat steaks may take some effort, but you might feel more prayerful. If you *can't* bring yourself to eat a completely plant-based diet, at least eat a healthy one that doesn't require too many of the earth's resources and doesn't harm your body. If you're a vegetarian, this will be an easy part of your prayer activity; if you're a piscetarian (a vegetarian who eats fish), then you'll be eating Jesus' own diet in Scripture.

Maybe you'd like to extend that idea when you pray-eat, and have a "biblical" dinner. Food in Jesus' time usually consisted of dates, figs, olives, curd cheese (farmer, hoop, or ricotta cheeses are close to what they eat in the Mediterranean region), harder cheeses, often from goat or sheep's milk but sometimes "cheese of kine,"[1] cow's milk. The people of the New Testament ate bread made from wheat, barley, meal, parched grain, beans, and lentils; and honey was always present. They included in their diet onions, leeks, melons, grapes, greens, and an occasional piece of fish. On holy days, Israelites ate lamb or kid, but the beef or poultry were used for sacrifices and were usually eaten only at major feasts. It's fun to invite friends to these Bible dinners: that way you get to pray while cooking *and* eating.

Celebrate the Food

Recently I bought eight china soup bowls at a garage sale, for a total of two dollars. I think food should look good, even if we're only serving soup. So I use those gorgeous bowls to celebrate the food and the people eating it. Your best china isn't just something for your daughter to inherit: use it often because it always signals "special," just as the chalice and paten do at Communion. It's no accident that most churches use silver or gold for the Eucharist: those are the church's way of declaring a celebration.

Set a beautiful table, with your best dishes and tablecloth and the silverware laid out properly. When you eat as prayer, the table and the food itself should reveal your intention and celebration by being attractive. The smell, taste, and look of food have a lot to do with digestion and enjoyment, and if you eat as a form of prayer, you need to have a good time doing it. So if you hate spinach or okra or salmon, don't try to eat them as a form of prayer or you'll learn to hate this activity. Eat healthy food, but eat what's pleasing to your palate.

How about treats? Famed cardiologist and nutrition specialist Dean Ornish, M.D, founder and president of the non-profit Preventive Medicine Research Institute in Sausalito, California, says, "And if you're going to eat chocolate (which I also enjoy), find a piece of the richest, darkest, most luscious chocolate and eat it as a form of meditation —savor it, spend a few minutes on even one piece. Then you'll get the sensual enjoyment without the excessive amounts that can lead to problems."[2] Those words describe eating as prayer, and when you can apply this description to every bite of all your food, you will have made strides toward holiness in your life.

Pray by Foraging

Years ago, I fell in love with Euell Gibbons's *Stalking the Wild Asparagus*[3] and his other books about foraging. There's something sacred and satisfying about gathering and preparing wild food. I love to bring home wild mustard greens and I know where to get chanterelle mushrooms in November. Currants and huckleberries grow wild in our hills, and in late summer, Oregon's landscape is overlaid by wild blackberry canes bearing the juiciest, darkest blackberries in the world. And in fall, big umbels of elderberries hang waiting for bears or jelly makers. (Elderberries make wonderful wine, too.) And since what grows wild seems closer to Eden, to the way God intended for us to live, foraging is a good way to pray.

"Wildman" Steve Brill was introduced to foraging in 1979, when he met up with a group of Greek women looking for fresh, wild ingredients in a New York park. Twenty-one years later, Brill is a professional naturalist and environmental educator who leads wild food and ecology tours in and around New York City. His six rules for foraging wild foods are:[4]

1. Identify every plant with 100-percent certainty.
2. Avoid species with poisonous look-alikes until you can distinguish between the two.
3. Collect small portions of common plants where they are very common.
4. Take only what you need without disturbing the habitat.
5. Avoid polluted soil and areas within fifty feet of heavy traffic or railroad lines.
6. Rinse everything thoroughly under running water and eat small amounts at first, in case of allergies or adverse reactions.

Several years ago, a friend and I went on an April foraging trip to the Oregon coast. We took some biscuit mix for coating and thickening, about a cup of vinegar, some canola oil, a little sugar, salt, and enough coffee for one day. Since we stayed for about five days, that meant we had to create "faux" teas and coffees that were tasty enough to substitute for the real thing.

We dug chicory roots and roasted them, then ground them for coffee. We made teas from salal and huckleberry leaves, and simmered the unopened buds of mustard plant as broccoli. Our salads contained miner's lettuce, pigweed, beach pea vine, boiled sea lettuce, and purslane.

Clams were available in the wet sand at low tide, and we cut fresh mussels off the pier pilings. We rented an ocean trap and spent a day crabbing; the fresh crabmeat was so good we could hardly eat it for laughing. We accompanied our seafood with salads, sand plums, dandelion fritters, and "broccoli" soup. And we flavored some of our foods with tiny slices of thick red seaweed and Oregon myrtlewood leaves, which taste like bay leaves. Since we were both on spiritual journeys as well as foraging, our days at the coast, looking for food but also basking on the sand or walking the surf line looking for seashells, were sacred experiences. And were we starving? All I can tell you is that I gained two pounds on the five-day trip!

Insights about Eating

Practitioners of yoga say that if we can offer our food to God with devotion before eating it, we can actually make spiritual progress by eating the offered food. Our devotion, and God's grace, transforms the food offered from material nutrition to spiritual mercy or what is in India called *prasada*. Yogis can't offer any onions, garlic, or mushrooms because their Vedic scriptures, according to Dr. Frank Gaetano Morales, Ph.D. in *Dharma Central*,[5] explain that these foods "excite the more passionate elements of the human psycho-physical constitution." The goal is to prepare delicious foods, not with our own satisfaction in mind, but thinking of the satisfaction of God. Therefore, God should be the first to taste the fruits of our labors.

Charles MacInerny, a yoga and meditation teacher, includes some "food as meditation" pages on his web site. One method is "amnesia," where you pretend to yourself that you've tasted, say, a strawberry. See his instruction at http://www.yogateacher.com/text/meditation/on-line/eating.html.

His second method is "sincere appreciation," which is much like Dr. Ornish's meditation on chocolate and can be used when you're teaching kids to pray-eat.

Dr. David Simon, an endocrinologist who conducts seminars with Deepak Chopra, offers a number of ways to make eating a wisdom experience. He tells us always to eat in a settled environment. If you are eating in chaotic surroundings, he thinks, you are metabolizing the chaos along with the food. He also says to avoid watching violent television while eating dinner. His mundane-sounding advice—to enjoy your meals in silence or with people that you love—actually contains a profound idea for modern Americans who almost never get to eat every meal that way. Can you have silence at a deli, or a faddish restaurant? Do you eat at home with the TV or radio on?[6]

When you use food as prayer, be hungry and stop eating when you are comfortably full. Even if you were raised with the edict to "clean your plate," say "Amen," blow out your candle, and clear the table before you're stuffed. Try to eat slowly enough to really, *really* taste the food and, if you're eating with others, to enjoy their company. Eating as prayer never shuts out others, even if you don't tell them what you're doing. Let your loving treatment of your meal partners become one more offering to God.

Another writer, John Robbins, author of *Diet for a New America,* says that if you want to make a difference in the world, want to be a healing influence, you have to reach inward first.

"Food is the entry point to the project of taking responsibility for yourself in the world," he says. He suggests that if you eat with conscience and concern for others (including other creatures) you've taken a step toward healing our broken world. He adds, "Turns out it's the same diet that is best for us that also takes the least toll on the biosphere, conserves the resources that make food production possible, and causes the least amount of pollution, soil erosion, and deforestation. This plant-based diet allows the most land, energy, water, and labor to be available to other people, and causes the least suffering to animals. I mean, this is phenomenal. It's saying that what serves you serves others, too. You don't have to choose between what's good for you and what's good for others. When you do what is really, essentially, truthfully good for you, you're also doing what is good for the planet and other people, and the future."[7] Not everyone feels suited to the plant-based diet recommended by Robbins and Ornish and by practitioners of eastern religions. I eat meat, eggs, and cheese and sometimes butter. And on Thanksgiving whipped cream. But I do so *reverently.*

In the old movie *Cool Hand Luke,* the protagonist—an inmate in a corrupt prison system—played by Paul Newman, says he can eat fifty hard-boiled eggs. His fellow prisoners took bets and made big preparations in a party-like atmosphere, and Luke became a kind of hero to them. Luke wasn't eating for satisfaction, but to prove a point and win a bet. I like to joke that if they were *deviled* eggs, I might be able to eat fifty. But stuff myself with that much food at one time? And all one kind of food?

Sometimes I probably ingest more calories than I need. I know that at one sitting, I can consume a whole bag of potato chips or an entire box of chocolates because I like the taste. I know this: self-indulgent overeating, whether the meal is a luscious duck confit or plain green soy beans, isn't a holy occupation. And since we're hoping for holiness, and care about the earth we live on, we must make some new decisions about food. Or we might all turn into velociraptors.

A Prayer for Eating

Bless this food to our use, gracious God. Help us to remember those who have nothing to eat today, and give us the wisdom to do something about that. Amen

CHAPTER THIRTEEN

The Wedding Banquet

"... Blessed are those who are invited to the marriage supper of the Lamb." And he said to me, "These are true words of God."—Revelation 19:9

You have eaten *as* prayer; now you can eat prayer itself, be part of a feast that contains the bread of life. And as you eat, you practice for a great celebration.

Practice is an important part of learning. I once had a kitten that grew up to be the greatest hunter in Oregon, possibly in the country. He stalked, he pounced, he devoured when he could. The problem was that he hunted *me*. When I was cooking, he would sneak to the top of the refrigerator and dive down onto my back, claws extended. As I loaded the washing machine he grabbed my ankles and bit them, and he leapt into the bathtub once, trying to take my leg as a trophy. (He at least never tried that one again.) He also deviled my peaceful little dog, pouncing, scratching, and yowling.

His assaults on me and my dog were *rehearsal*. He was learning to jump on a moving target and sink his teeth and claws into his possible dinner or enemy. When he was big enough, he gave up his attacks on us and headed into the backyard where he fought with the squirrels (at a distance; he was a smart cat) and seized voles, mice, and the poor little birds that got in his path. He came over the fence with snakes and lizards, and he once shook a baby rattler till its neck snapped.

Dress Rehearsal

Christians practice every Sunday, and sometimes on weekdays. When the celebrant says, "In the night on which he was betrayed, our Lord took bread . . ." the practice session starts. And when we eat the bread and sip the wine, we've performed a dress rehearsal for the real banquet that will take place someday—the marriage feast of Christ to his bride, the Church. We need training for that banquet, because using the wrong fork wouldn't matter, but appearing in less than a spotless garment could.

Whether you accept a literal Second Coming and *parousia* and Armageddon, or think that the Book of Revelation describes the inner, spiritual struggle of all Christians, or even suspect that Revelation is gibberish and shouldn't have been allowed into the Canon, we all believe in some kind of Christian Culmination. Earth and society will probably not go on forever, especially with the present rate of pollution and warming. And most Christians think that God intends us to attend a final event in time, one in which Christ is victorious. So we hold the marriage supper of the Lamb in our minds as a collective belief about the end of time and the entrance into eternity. If you didn't believe in that end, you probably wouldn't find so much meaning in Communion. You could sleep till afternoon on Sundays, and grill hamburgers for dinner without a thought of Christ. But because you went forward and knelt at the altar, because you said, "Therefore let us keep the feast," you told God you wanted to be part of not only that morning's celebration but hoped also to be present at Christ's great nuptial dinner.

The Eucharist is the centerpiece of our worship, and it changes us. I once approached God in a sort of cranky mood, saying why couldn't I have the overwhelming experiences at Communion as some others? Catherine of Sienna not only received the stigmata at Eucharist, but she fell into a swoon during which she saw God in action. Teresa of Avila and Padre Pio are supposed to have levitated at Communion. Gabrielle Bossis, author of *He and I,* had amazing experiences at the altar rail.[1] So why couldn't I?

I think there was a silence in heaven, maybe a half hour. I was doing something different: cracking pecans or watering plants or quarreling with my cat, when I heard God's voice in my heart.

"Where do you think you got your faith?" God said. "You've been taking communion since you were eleven years old, and each time I sent you a greater gift of faith."

I stood in that same spot for a long time. I *had* received stigmata: faith marked my hands and feet and brow and heart. Sweet injury! I did not bleed, but the gift of faith informs my life. And though God didn't call me to be a missionary in India or to evangelize the unchurched, God has asked me to write and talk about faith to those who are in the church. And faith, faith I can tell you about, is the gift I've received over and over and over again while I practiced for the Marriage Supper of the Lamb.

The Original Version

In ancient Israel, a man who wanted to marry had to first obtain his father's permission. Usually the father and son visited the bride's family together, and if the father of the groom found the girl worthy, they paid a price for her. The bride-price not only allayed the expense of having the bad luck to raise a girl, but also was a sign of the groom's love. That bride-price was the most important part of the marriage contract. So the young man would go to the girl's house with the contract, and present his offer to her and her father. And if a previous marriage contract existed but had not been consummated, the bridegroom had to give a ransom or forfeit to satisfy the previous suitor.

If the girl's father agreed to the bride-price, the bridegroom would pour a glass of wine. If she drank the wine, she showed the groom that she accepted his proposal. At this point, the couple was counted as legally betrothed, which was as legally binding as a marriage. During this time the bride and bridegroom might not see each other, but they exchanged messages of love while the groom was preparing a place for her.

After the wine, the bridegroom presented the bride with special gifts, to show his love for her and to help her to remember him during the long betrothal period. Sometimes there was a small celebration feast, and then the bridegroom departed to build a beautiful bridal chamber, usually in his father's house. And this is important: *only his father decided when the chamber was finished.*

While the bridegroom was preparing the wedding chamber, the bride was considered to be consecrated, set apart or "bought with a price." If she went out, she would wear a veil so others would know she was betrothed. During this time she prepared herself for the marriage.

Finally, when the bridal chamber was finished, the groom would "kidnap" his bride. The occasion was prearranged, though nobody knew the exact day and hour when he would arrive; they only knew that when the bridegroom's father gave permission for the wedding to take place, he would come. No doubt, gossip helped alert the bride that her new home was ready and she would begin her preparations.

She would have to have a *mikvah,* or ritual bath before the event, then clothe herself in a new gown, one made of linen only with no other threads woven into it. Then the bride and her maids would wait up every night, perhaps falling asleep, until a servant outdoors would shout, "The bridegroom comes!" The bridesmaids would jump to their feet and trim their lamps, and the groom would sneak into the house, "like a thief in the night,"[2] carrying away his new wife. Of course, everyone—the bridesmaids, the groomsmen, the parents on both sides, and all the neighbors—would all follow the lamps through the night to the wedding feast at the bridegroom's father's home.

While the family and friends celebrated and feasted, the bridal couple spent seven days in the new bridal chamber, learning how to love each other. Finally, they would emerge on the last day of the feast, and take part in the celebration.

Christ Woos His Bride

Jesus came to earth, the home of his bride, and offered his marriage contract. That contract is the New Covenant, written in his blood, and it not only provides for the forgiveness of sins, but makes us the object of his love.

Jesus paid the bride-price with his life. At the Last Supper, breaking bread, he revealed the price he was paying: ". . . This is my body given for you. . . ." He died as a ransom, or forfeit, to set humanity free from the sins committed under the first covenant, the Law of Moses. Christ woos his bride, the Church.

Just as a cup of wine sealed the marriage contract, so Jesus offered the cup of wine to his disciples, and described the covenant to them: "Then he took a cup, and after giving thanks he gave it to them, saying, 'Drink from it, all of you; for this is the New Covenant in my blood.'"

Once we drink from that cup, we are betrothed, which is a much more binding condition than a modern engagement. If we wander away from that betrothal, we're committing spiritual adultery, and though we can obtain forgiveness from all our sins, they at least temporarily separate us from our Bridegroom.

Jesus himself did not drink, just as a bridegroom at the ancient betrothal did not. He told his disciples, "I tell you, I will never again drink of this fruit of the vine until that day when I drink it new with you in my Father's kingdom." In other words, "I will drink wine only with you, at our marriage banquet."

The gift that Jesus gave his Bride is the Holy Spirit, who guides and teaches us throughout our lives. Sometimes the Holy Spirit moves on a grand scale: in one year we saw the downfall of Marxism, the breaching of the Berlin wall, the great changes in South Africa (who would ever, *ever* have believed that Nelson Mandela would not only walk out of prison, but be elected president of South Africa?). Sometimes the Spirit brings smaller gifts of insight or understanding, but irrespective of size, the earth without the Holy Spirit would be a barren, sad planet with even more trouble than it already has.

Like the Jewish bridegroom, Jesus is preparing a place for us. "And if I go and prepare a place for you, I will come again and will take you to myself, so that where I am, there you may be also. " And just as a father in biblical times was the only one who could decide when the bridal chamber was ready, Jesus said, "But about that day and hour no one knows, neither the angels of heaven, nor the Son, but only the Father" (Matthew 24:36).

And Jesus will "kidnap" his bride in the night: "For you yourselves know very well that the day of the Lord will come like a thief in the night" (1 Thessalonians 5:2).

Like brides in biblical times, the Church has to be ready for her wedding. Our *mikvah* is baptism, which John the Baptist performed with water, and in which Jesus immerses us with the Holy Spirit. And then comes the wedding banquet, the Marriage Feast of the Lamb. For seven "days," we will bask in Christ's love, just as a Jewish bride and groom spent a week alone in the wedding chamber, while the others feasted and celebrated. Finally on the last day of the feast—the day Jesus blessed with his first miracle—we will emerge and discover that the last day of the celebration is forever. And that celebration will be greater than any on earth.

Revelation says, "For the wedding of the Lamb has come, and his bride has made herself ready. Fine linen, bright and clean, was given her to wear." (Fine linen stands for the righteous acts of the saints.) Then the angel said to me, "'Write: 'Blessed are those who are invited to the wedding supper of the Lamb!'"

So keep your lamps trimmed and your linen wedding dress clean. Any minute now, like a thief in the night, you might hear the shout of an angel and the blowing of the ceremonial Jewish ram's horn, or *shofar.* Jesus said to stay awake, which doesn't mean you have to give up sleeping in case of the Coming, but to be spiritually awake and aware, prepared for heaven (no matter where you think heaven is).

Even if you believe that most of this prophecy is symbolic, it's important to keep the faith. Such a huge Christian collective exists that we need to let Christ complete his "hero's journey" in us. He is more than a psychic reality: Paul Tillich, existentialist theologian, often spoke of Jesus as "ground of our being."[3] And if you have skipped the Eucharist lately, go to church and receive the Body and Blood. Thich Nhat Hanh, the Buddhist scholar, comments that the elements, which *must* be perceived as being the actual Body and Blood, are meant to resurrect us, to flood us with new life and strength.[4]

If a Buddhist sees the truth of our liturgy and our wedding feast rehearsal, then we as Christians can respond with even more enthusiasm. We are *invited* to the marriage supper, to the culmination, to becoming one with Christ.

Getting Started

My husband and I like to make a point of ordering a glass of wine and some kind of bread when we eat out, and we consume it before dinner so the rest of the meal is an extension of our *agape*. At home, that same kind of "little communion" makes the half-glass of red wine my doctor prescribed into a lovely celebration of Christ's love for his bride.

You can create small "wedding banquets" at home or anywhere; if you're a purist, you should use grape wine and wheat bread, but I love remembering a retreat where the offering was rice crackers and strawberry pop, and it was as holy as any other I've attended.

A Prayer for the Banquet

So as you sit down with a spouse or friend or offspring to eat bread and drink wine, you might say as a prayer the words of John Donne:

> Batter my heart, three personed-God . . .
> Take me to you, imprison me, for I
> Except you 'enthrall me, never shall be free,
> Nor ever chaste, except you ravish me. [5]

CHAPTER FOURTEEN

Sacred and Secret

You desire truth in the inward being; therefore teach me wisdom in my secret heart. —Psalm 51:6

But whenever you pray, go into your room and shut the door and pray to your Father who is in secret; and your Father who sees in secret will reward you. —Matthew 6:6

When I walk through my house, I usually nod to several "altars," spots where I have hidden something: a tiny china bird to symbolize the Holy Spirit is secreted behind encyclopedias in my entry hall's tall book case, and a little wooden cross wrapped in pink paper is under the washing machine. On my dresser, a tiny silver container holds an even tinier angel. A small terra-cotta replica of an Incan jaguar altar hides behind an antique pitcher in my living room, to remind me of Christ's ultimate sacrifice. A cockle shell in the drawer of my bedside table proclaims that my life is pilgrimage.[1] A dark, sea-tumbled rock lies quietly in a small red bag in my office, to help me recall a life-changing retreat, and Ganeesh, the Hindu elephant God of wisdom, hides in a silver sugar bowl, reminding me that all wisdom and power come from God, the God of Scripture, and are available through prayer.[2]

Nobody else—except my best friend, and now you—knows about these tiny worship spots, and none of the hidden symbols is an altar itself (except the jaguar). I have to use my mind to bank the imaginary altar with roses or lilies, to light candles in a tall stand, to swing a silver thurible full of smoking frankincense. The symbols are hidden reminders; my inner eye creates the worship. A trip from my office to the kitchen can sometimes have several stops to pray, chant, sing a hymn, or drop for a moment to my right knee in adoration of God, and in thanksgiving for his coming to earth as Jesus Christ.

I think my secret "altars," and my acknowledging them, may be the best prayers I do. I don't link them to other experiences or other meanings, and I don't pray them to impress anyone. They are purely reminders of my desperate need to worship.

Some altars are hidden in plain sight: a hunk of quartz with a large garnet in the corner is the paperweight on my desk. Nobody knows (at least until now) that the rock reminds me that "there is gold, and abundance of costly stones; but the lips informed by knowledge are a precious jewel" (Proverbs 20:15). Many more small garnets jut out of the coppery pyrite on the back of the quartz. Since the garnet is my birthstone, I get to thank God for my life every time I look at the paperweight.

I've often thought that maybe the "New Agers" who meditate with crystals borrowed the exercise from us, as they did so many other activities like contemplation and chanting. Crystals aren't poison: crystals and gems, engraved with the names of the twelve tribes, were in Aaron's breastplate of judgment, which he wore in the holiest place before the Lord; according to Revelation, the walls of the New Jerusalem were adorned with those same kinds of engraved jewels. God had named gems to be instruments of religion and spirituality.

Crystals are a mysterious force. They're never "done"; they grow, although much more slowly than we can perceive. One crystal might grow a thousandth of a millimeter in twenty years, but another might take a million years to enlarge the same amount. I think they're one of God's secrets. Gems and crystals somehow fit into God's scheme, so I have a secret awe for God through my quartz-and-garnet rock.

I don't go so far as to gaze into a crystal ball, but I've mentioned that when the afternoon sun on the prisms that hang in my bedroom window sends scraps of the rainbow all over the room, I worship. The sign of God's very first covenant with humanity was the rainbow, and rainbows are just arcane enough to be that divine hologram. The rainbow covenant was, on its surface, about floods, but the deeper meaning is that God thinks we are important enough to receive a promise and a sign—a revelation of God's nature, a glimpse of a greater mystery. So like all symbols of worship, whether they be jaguars or Celtic crosses, crystals and rainbow, they are not only my secret but God's. We share it together.

And I think God enjoys having secrets with us, secret prayers, secret pacts, and mysterious qualities. Jesus talked about the secrets of the kingdom of God, and said that when we pray to our Father who is in secret, our Father who sees in secret will reward us. Deuteronomy 29:29 says, "The secret things belong to the Lord our God, but the revealed things belong to us and to our children forever, to observe all the words of this law." Jesus was God's secret for who-knows-how-many thousands or millions or billions of years. The mysteries of Christianity that have been revealed to us are "things into which angels long to look!"[3]

Why have a secret prayer life? First of all, to keep from showing off. When I look back at my life, the incidents that make me (and probably my children) cringe with shame are the times when I thought I was making an impression, or dramatizing my own importance. (I have to confess to the reader that I just blushed.) Jesus talked about doing your alms before men, and although you may fold your pledge check before you drop it in the plate, you might, like me, be tempted to look like a hard worker, or act hip to theology, or present yourself as a Bible expert. So I avoid telling people I meet at church that I'm a writer. I think bragging doesn't belong to kingdom life, and showing off is the first step on a path to the pit. So when I worship secretly, I'm not doing my alms before men *or* women and I'm not displaying my immense holiness so people will admire me.

And what goes on in secret is unrestricted. I probably shouldn't stand up in church and wave my arms like a bird, or sing a solo, or dance in a circle; but I can do all those things, and more, in secret, and God, who sees in secret, always sends me a dollop of love. When I think about my jaguar altar, I can tap dance or howl or sing, all things

I wouldn't do in public. One day I grabbed a dishtowel and used it as a sort of dance veil, swinging it over my head while I skipped and slid and sang, "I love you, God."

Being secret helps make a lot of things sacred. Unless I use a set prayer, I am not crazy about praying aloud with a group because I can hear myself, and be tempted to become publicly eloquent. And when others pray aloud, their prayers sometimes sound like sermonettes for the others in the group more than like a message to God. So when I lead retreats or spirituality groups, I like to tell participants that we'll keep silence while they *write* their prayers of petition or intercession or adoration in their notebooks, which they can keep and look back at. That way, we don't engage in rambling prayers or group sentence prayers that can at best be lengthy and at worst dwindle away into what Father William McNamara called "spooky sighs and husky hums."[4] I usually keep group prayer in our Prayer Book or similar sources. That way, nobody has to bare his or her soul or mention her husband's gambling and her sister's bitter marriage. The notebook becomes the "secret place" where Jesus told us to go, and pray.

Sometimes you can take a wild, secret action and push it into prayer. On my birthday twenty years ago, I got in my car while my husband was at a conference, and I drove to Cape Kiwanda, about a hundred miles from here, where hang-gliders exercise their talents on sunny days and sometimes drizzly ones. I asked a young man with a silver glider to give me a lesson; when he said no, I waved a hundred-dollar bill in his face and he rethought. When the time came for me to solo, I panicked.

"I don't remember what to do!" I said and he smiled.

"Don't do anything," he said. "Do nothing. Let the wind and the glider do it." I lay across the bar and did nothing, and I sailed out over the surf like Daedelus, and then I remembered how to make the glider turn and I came down on the beach. I did that three times, and when I got back in my car, I felt as if I'd been lost in prayer for ten days. I wasn't scared until afterward, when I realized that hang-gliding isn't a safe sport for amateurs. But what a prayer it was! The quiet was amazing; I could hear the ocean roar beneath me, but faintly, removed. I was alone in space, I flew like an albatross, I had been only a few inches from God's heart; in fact, I think it was God's breath that held me in the air while I did nothing at all.

I kept that adventure secret for about a year, partly because I knew my husband would be horrified and lecture me, and partly because I wanted to shelter the experience within me. Sometimes our prayer adventures are fragile. Once you release them from memory into the world, they can get battered and bruised. I knew that when I told anyone, they'd want to know about the gliding and the glider, and for me the experience was spiritual. When I finally did mention my hang-gliding in a sermon I preached, my husband was so dumfounded he said he thought I made it up!

Mystical secrets aren't the same as temporal ones. I don't hide receipts from the bookstore or boxes from Amazon.com from my husband. I don't have any secret charge accounts, and I certainly don't have any extramarital experiences. But sometimes an adventure of the spirit, even if it's just hiding a little cross in a place nobody but you knows about, needs to be nurtured in silence.

When Jesus was a baby, his parents fled to Egypt to protect him. He was hidden, a secret from all but a few. After they took him to the Temple, Mary and Joseph told nobody about the shepherds, the Wise Men, and the angels in the sky. The Christ Child didn't play in the streets of Jerusalem or Bethlehem, and didn't begin his ministry until he was a grown man. And it's the same way with some spiritual experiences: you may need to wait until they're mature before you reveal them to your world. You can slowly tell your spouse or kids or best friends about some of your hidden altars, but keep some of them private.

Getting Started

Secrets are fun when they're nice ones. They make "doing prayer" a little bit exciting, as you choose objects, or even tiny scrolls with Scripture or other quotes on them, and decide where to put them every day. If you start with only one hidden reminder to worship, you can then enlarge your territory, a little at a time, until every corner of every room makes you smile or bow as an offering to God.

A Prayer for Secret Worship

Jesus, you told us to pray in our secret place. Help me to recall my secret places, and give me a real sense of worship. Amen

CHAPTER FIFTEEN

Beyond Doing

Be still, and know that I am God! I am exalted among the nations, I am exalted in the earth. —Psalm 46:10

The Red Queen in *Through the Looking Glass* said she had learned to imagine six impossible things before breakfast every day and wanted Alice to try it. If I had her here with me, I would argue that, because in imagination *nothing* is impossible, her statement was a contradiction of itself. Imagination is the door to adventure, and never limited by numbers. Even if you were chained to a wall in a dungeon, you could, in imagination, run through a field of dandelions. Or juggle flaming swords. Or talk to God face to face. Or any number of amazing events; why stop at six? A few things may have been enough for the Red Queen, but the person who longs for God and is learning to "do" prayer uses imagination in every second of prayer, done or spoken.

Imagination doesn't get a good review in the Bible. The few references I found for "imagination" or "imagine" were negative. Prophets especially sounded mad when they said rich men imagine that their wealth is a strong wall of protection, or that the people imagine a vain thing. But I think that's because God gave us imagination as a precious gift and is offended by the way people sometimes use it to start wars, commit murders and rapes, first in their minds and then in the flesh (the law calls that "premeditation"). People insult God when they imagine themselves heading into better circumstances without doing the work necessary. The *worst* thing that Scripture suggests is to imagine we can do anything on our own, without God's assistance.

The Image of God

We are created in the image of God. That doesn't mean God is my height or my age or has very, very fine hair like mine. It means God imbued us with God's nature, including thought and intellect and imagination. I suspect that imagination is *so* important that it might be a sin to misuse it. That doesn't mean an odd thought that hops through your consciousness is bad; but play with that temptation in your mind, visualize something you know you shouldn't do, and you're turning yourself into something you won't like in the end. I think the gift of imagination is a lot like the gift of sex: *because* it's so wonderful and powerful, you need to use it carefully and with reverence.

Does that mean you can only imagine religious things? That you should turn off your fantasies unless they contain pictures of Jesus or heaven? Of course not. Today as I stood under the awning in my patio, drinking my favorite Yorkshire tea and letting my mind have its way, I suddenly imagined I heard Jimi Hendrix playing the "Star Spangled Banner" at Woodstock; and I laughed out loud. I realized in a moment that what I had heard was a swallow—we have two swallow families in the eaves of our garage—scolding my little dog in a sliding, almost nasal voice. But my mind continued its free fall and converted the swallow back into the guitar player standing on the stage with a dark red tie around his head, his instrument hanging almost against his hip, and an audience of flower children screaming their approval. When he suddenly grew a beak and his fringed white sleeves turned into wings, I laughed out loud again and I took my empty teacup indoors. Imagination and memory had united to give me a glimpse of at least one possible thing. Fantasy is the one thing nobody but I can control; nobody else can see or hear or taste what I do in imagination. This is beyond doing. Instead of the linear thinking produced by my frontal lobe, I let a deeper part of my brain range free, climbing unscalable mountains and swimming at the deepest part of the ocean. The reason I think imagination is such a precious gift to human beings is because during my exercise of the possible, I am freed from the bindings of everyday life. And when I am free I am close to that thin membrane that's like the Stargate: I can throw myself through into God's presence.

My good friend loves to pull weeds in her back yard while she daydreams. She writes mentally, imagining new chapters to her novel or an article for a magazine. She imagines her troubled son with a steady job and a girlfriend instead of the voices and urges that torment him. She plans activities that may never take place and sees the world at peace. She and I argue about her practice: I think you should do what you're doing, and I say she's fragmenting herself; that when she pulls weeds, she should think about pulling weeds. But she says that daydreaming is a form of prayer and refreshes her more than anything. We haven't yet settled this use of the imagination, but if she sees it as prayer, then I know God honors her practice.

A Pure Mind

Gautama Siddhartha, the Buddha, said, "What we are today comes from our thoughts of yesterday, and our present thoughts build our life of tomorrow: Our life is the creation of our mind. If a man speaks or acts with an impure mind, suffering follows him as the wheel of the cart follows the beast that draws the cart. If a man speaks or acts with a pure mind, Joy follows him as his own shadow." What you're doing today is a product of yesterday's imagination.

But how do you get the "pure mind" that will determine the qualities of tomorrow?

I guess you have to ask. One of my favorite requests is the *Book of Common Prayer*'s collect for the fourth Sunday in Advent: "Purify our conscience, Almighty God, by your daily visitation, that your Son Jesus Christ, at his coming, may find in us a mansion prepared for himself; who lives and reigns with you in the unity of the Holy Spirit, one God, now and forever." Oh, yes, please yes, this time not a stable, not a cave full of animal warmth and odors, not a hiding place in

Egypt. Purify my conscience, God, so that what I build in my imagination isn't an easier life for myself but a palace for my King. I don't think "purify" means "don't read *Playboy*"; it means learning not to think about revenge or smart comebacks or sarcasm or fear or hopelessness. To be hopeless or afraid of the future is impure because it doubts God's help. Christian hope is one of the most important virtues your imagination can capture.

Sometimes at night I like to close my eyes and build that "mansion" for Christ. I love to imagine a dining table, and sometimes I choose a lavish menu. The steps to the porch are made of agate and the front door is one huge baroque pearl. And I usually try to give myself a modest servant's quarter, even though he keeps urging me to be his honored guest, his sister.

I also take my imagination to the front porch. I sit quietly where I can hear my fifteen wind chimes and I repeat a "breath prayer" or short phrase like "Jesus, Lord," and let my imagination take over. The words stop, and the sound of the wind bells fade as I move somewhere in my mind to where God is. I don't try to quench colors or music or the rare images that come to my mind's eye. I let God take me on a tour of my inner self, the one that only emerges in silence. I sometimes imagine standing on the rim of a volcano or that I'm swept up, like Elijah, in a whirlwind, where I am nearly deafened by the voice of God pronouncing God's own name.

Memory helps my spiritual imagination. I can remember a cave in the hills above my little hometown of Superior, Arizona, where seashells and other fossils protruded from the rocky walls. When I first went there—a place I was forbidden to go by my parents, who feared I might fall into a crevasse and die—I remember my awe at little limestone "raspberries" and perfectly preserved fish with pleated fins and tails, embedded in a layer of rose quartz. I like to "be" in that cave through remembering, so I can listen to the songs of ancient seacreatures who tell me about God, about creation, and about their waiting for the Resurrection. Sometimes I take Jesus with me, and we listen together and marvel at the music and the sight.

And in my imagination, I can fly, overcoming gravity as well as terror. I can swoop over forested mountains and crashing seas and deserts that are thick with wildflowers; I can fly straight to heaven, wherever that is, or circumnavigate the earth, asking God's blessing on its inhabitants. I love to imagine lying on the wind like Superman and speeding over the landscape, looking down at patchwork farms and oceans the color of sapphires and aquamarines. I even imagine that I can telescope my arm to get a can of paprika from a high shelf, or extend my leg twenty feet to test the temperature of a lake before I dive in.

I am never more free than when my mind takes flight into the mystery of God. Imagination not only protects but also *creates* freedom, and permits me to see God, high and lifted up, with seraphim darting about touching things and people with hot coals, with elders hurling down their crowns, with cherubim whose eyes are sleepless flying over the earth, wielding the swords that cut between soul and spirit.

Finally Being Still

Many religions and spiritual disciplines start with the premise that we are like God, and have simply forgotten; what we should do through prayer and meditation is to re-remember. But the Christian mind believes that we and God are made of different stuff, different substance; instead of remembering that we are God, we aspire to see God, know God, and be *like* God. And you find God in your own stillpoint, a place beyond thought or action or even awareness.

To be still is beyond *doing* prayer. It's *being* prayer. The Hebrew of God's command to be still and know is similar to *standing* still: stop what you're doing and know me. God is saying, *I need no more attention or sacrifice. Just be empty, and I will fill you. Stop your prayers, be prayer, and I will pray you. I will think through your mind and hear through your ears. I will live through you.*

The whole trick is to be still, and that's not the modern American way. We rush into prayer the same way we rush around doing everything else. But if God wants you to stand still, then you need to do it. And remember the words of Yoda, the wise and tiny creature from *Star Wars:* "There is no try. There is only do." So no matter how busy you are or how demanding your life is, try to do nothing and you'll learn to know God. But it ain't easy. So don't try to get there all at once. Begin with a minute or two every day where you sit or lie or stand still (without falling asleep) and empty your mind. You may get into stillness by sitting, Zen-style, where you acknowledge every thought that jumps into your head, but you don't follow it it, you let the thought pass by. Don't use a prayer or a mantra because that might lead you into ideas. Let your imagination fly away or sleep while you try to become nobody so God can become, through you, a reality. If you begin to feel anxious, stop: this is as far as you can go that day with *kenosis,* or emptying. Of course, unlike Zen practitioners who empty because to be empty is virtuous, your goal is to empty yourself in order to be filled with God.

If sitting in silence makes you more jumpy than prayerful, try some rhythmic activity. The place where I can achieve kenosis is swimming. Something about the water and my body's gliding through it empties my mind. I love water; I could happily live in a world that was water at least to my waist, and sometimes I just stand in the pool for a while before I start to swim. When I get out and dry off, I have done prayer without thinking prayer, usually without intention. In the water I have allowed God to have a greater portion of my mind and soul, and my hope is that eventually I'll be so filled by God that I am suffused by divinity. Not so I can be puffed up because I am so suffused, but to be humbled by love.

And love is what all these prayer-doings are about. You walked and danced and painted as an offering to the Most High, not because God demanded worship and praise, but because you love God and wanted to express that love. Love is beyond doing: if you're a paraplegic or cannot speak, you can still love God and ask God to live in you, to be the arms and legs you can't use, to show you a world you can't get out to see.

And if you *can* move your body, then God can teach you to imagine and laugh, to see with new eyes and dance with new feet. God has not created you to be a servant, but a son or daughter in the royal house. Your doing prayer is a way for you and God to live together in joy.

Afterthought

By now, you've certainly thought of new ways to do your prayers. Keep track of them in a journal, and try to form some "doing prayer" groups among your friends because when two or three are gathered together in his name, Christ is among you.

Notes

Chapter One

1. Norman Pittinger, *Praying Today: Practical Thoughts on Prayer* (Grand Rapids, Mich.: William B. Eerdmans Publishing Company, 1974).

2. Francine Prose, *Household Saints* (New York: St. Martin's Press, 1981).

3. "God Be in My Head," from the 1538 *Sarum Primer*. "Sarum Use" is the name applies to the particular rendering of divine worship in the English Church that was developed at Salisbury, in Wiltshire, from the early thirteenth century, a local expression of the Western or Roman Rite in England up to the Reformation. "Sarum" is the abbreviation of "Sarisburium," the Latin word for Salisbury, which was and is both a city and a diocese in south central England. Words: *Sarum Primer,* 1538; Music; God be in my head, by Sidney Lytlington, (1875–1947); Meter: Irregular. "God Be in My Head" is # 694 in the Episcopal Hymnbook 1982, ©1985 by The Church Pension Fund, 800 Second Ave. New York, NY 10017.

Chapter Two

1. Thich Nhat Hanh, *The Miracle of Mindfulness* (Boston: Beacon, 1996), 26.

2. Quoted in Frank Waters, *The Book of the Hopi* (New York: Penguin Books, 1985), 52.

Chapter Three

1. Lauren Artress, *Walking a Sacred Path: Rediscovering the Labyrinth as a Spiritual Tool* (New York: Riverhead Books, 1996).
2. Frank Waters, *Book of the Hopi*. 52.
3. "One Step at a Time" by Suzanne Moody. Copyright © 1999 by Suzanne Moody. All rights reserved. Used by permission of the author.

Chapter Four

1. Founded by the philosopher and writer Mevlana Celaleddin Rumi in the thirteenth century, the ritual of the Mevlevi sect, also known as the "sema," is a serious religious ritual performed by Sufi Muslim priests in a prayer trance to Allah. Mevlevi believed that during the sema the soul was released from earthly ties to freely and jubilantly commune with nature.
2. Iris Stewart, *Sacred Woman, Sacred Dance: Awakening Spirituality Through Movement and Ritual* (Rochester, Vt.: Inner Traditions International, Ltd., 2000).
3. Christy Edwards-Ronning, "Renew A Right Spirit Within Me: How Leaders Can Encourage a Worshipful Presence in their Dancers," Sacred Dance Guild, www.us.net/sdg/Renew.html.
4. "Heyschasm" refers to the spirituality which was characteristic of the Desert Fathers or contemplation in the Byzantine tradition; eremitical contemplation.
5. The dancer is Sharon Weldon, whose husband, the Rev. Jonathan Weldon, is rector of The Episcopal Church of the Resurrection.
6. "Herzliebster Jesu," by Johann Heerman (1585–1647); music by by Johann. Cruger (1598–1662). Hymn 158, The Hymnbook 1982, © 1985 by The Church Pension Fund, 800 Second Ave. New York, NY 10017.
7. Yehuda Berg, *The 72 Names of God: Technology for the Soul* (Los Angeles: Kabbalah Publishing, 2003), 60–61.
8. Ronald W. Clark, *Einstein: The Life and Times* (New York: Avon, 1999), 422.

Chapter Six

1. This fact is documented by speech therapists and physicians.

Chapter Seven

1. Edna St. Vincent Millay, "Renascence," in *Collected Poems of Edna St. Vincent Millay* (New York: Harper and Row, 1945), 3.

2. Thich Nhat Hanh, *Living Buddha, Living Christ* (New York: Riverhead Books, 1997), 16.

3. al-Ghazzali, *Essential Sufism*, ed. James Fadiman and Robert Frager (San Francisco: HarperSanFrancisco, 1998), 102.

Chapter Eight

1. St. John Damascene, *De Imaginis*, 1, 27; cited in CCC 1162. www.opus angelorum.org/Formation/Angelsandliturgy.html.

2. "Write" is the term traditionally used to describe the making of an icon, rather than "paint," perhaps because the icon contains a story or message; therefore, you "read" an icon as prayer in a picture.

3. The Mandelyon is not the Shroud of Turin. Other legends say it is the cloth with which St. Veronica wiped Jesus' face on the way to the cross.

4. "Jesus Christ, Son of God, have mercy on me sinner." This prayer has been used in the Russian church for at least two centuries and is said to contain the entire Gospel. In this case, it is used as a centering device.

5. Henri Nouwen, *Behold the Beauty of the Lord: Praying with Icons* (Notre Dame, Ind.: Ave Maria Press, 1987), 10.

6. Nouwen went to live at l'Arche the last years of his life.

7. Miriam K. Freund, *Jewels for a Crown: The Story of the Chagall Windows* (New York: McGraw-Hill, 1963).

8. P. Pfeiifer, *Meister Eckhardt* (vol. 2; London: C. de B. Evans, 1924), 80.

9. Available online at www.Autobahnkirche.de/spirit-container/alltagsexerzitien/grundkurs-engl/hw-c.htm#beginning.

Chapter Nine

1. Marshall McLuhan, et al, *The Medium is the Massage* (Madera, Calif.: Ginko Press Inc., 2001).

2. "Study suggests life sprang from clay," www.cnn.com/2003/TECH/science/10/25/clay.life.reut/.

3. "Thrown" clay has been tossed until the air bubbles are out of it.

4. Pamela Bloom, "The Bearable Lightness of Petals," in *Spirituality and Health: The Soul-Body Connection* (Fall 2000): 49.

Chapter Ten

1. Pamela Bloom, "The Bearable Lightness of Petals," in *Spirituality and Health: The Soul-Body Connection* (Fall 2000): 49.

Chapter Eleven

1. Acts 15:29; 1 Corinthians 8; Revelation 2:20; others.

2. "Prayer for the Home" is an ancient Omaha Indian Prayer. From Beliefnet.com, http://www.beliefnet.com/prayeroftheday/prayer_one.asp?pid =1961 (accessed November 25, 2003).

Chapter Twelve

1. See 1 Samuel 10:29 (KJV).

2. Dean Ornish, http://content.health.msn.com/content/article/60/67084.htm.

3. Euell Gibbons, *Stalking the Wild Asparagus* (Chambersburg, Pa.: Alan C. Hood & Co., 1987).

4. "Wildman" Steve Brill posts this list, information, and recipes for wild foods, and other foraging suggestions on his web page, www.wildmanstevebrill.com. He has guested on cable television's Food Channel.

5. Frank Gaetana Morales, "Eating as Meditation: How to Prepare Prasada," http://www.dharmacentral.com/articles/prasada.htm.

6. David Simon, M.D., *The Wisdom of Healing: A Natural Mind Body Program for Optimal Wellness* (New York: Three Rivers Press, 1998).

7. John Robbins, *Diet for a New America: How Your Food Choices Affect Your Health, Happiness and the Future of Life on Earth* (Tiburon, Calif.: H J Kramer, Inc., 1987), 227.

Chapter Thirteen

1. Gabrielle Bossis, *He and I* (Minneapolis, Minn.: The Daughters of St. Paul, Pauline Books and Media, 1988).

2. See 2 Peter 3:10 (KJV)

3. Paul Tillich, *Dynamics of Faith* (New York: Harper Perennial, 2001), 71.

4. Thich Nhat Hanh, *Living Buddha, Living Christ* (New York: Riverhead Books, 1997), 30–31.

5. John Clifford Grierson, *Metaphysical Lyrics & Poems of the Seventeenth Century, Donne to Butler* (Oxford: Clarendon, 1921), 51.

Chapter Fourteen

1. At the beginning of their pilgrimage, travelers who walk the route from a cathedral in Lyon, France, to the chapel of Santiago de Compostela, Spain, receive a scallop, or cockle shell, with a string to hang it around their necks. The tradition probably sprang from the need for something to scoop water from streams and fountains on the way. French chefs invented Coquille Saint Jacque (Scallops St. James) to use up the raw scallops.

2. Ganeesh isn't divine in my worship, but only a reminder that Jesus is the giver of wisdom. "If any of you is lacking in wisdom, ask God, who gives to all generously and ungrudgingly, and it will be given you" (James 1:5). Likewise, the jaguar altar tells me that Christ made the one perfect and sufficient sacrifice.

3. See 1 Peter 1:12.

4. William McNamara, OCD, *Mystical Passion: The Art of Christian Loving* (San Francisco: Harper & Row, 1979), 79.